STUDY GUIDE

Blessed Hope

The Book of Revelation

W. Robert Godfrey

LIGONIER MINISTRIES

Renew your Mind.

LIGONIER.ORG | 800-435-4343

421 Ligonier Court, Sanford, FL 32771
Email: info@ligonier.org

Printed in China.

Contents

Introduction

The book of Revelation offers a rich vision of blessing and encouragement to God's people in every generation. Given to a church struggling to reconcile the hope of Christ's reign with the harsh realities of life in a fallen world, this book continues to speak to believers today. In this teaching series, Dr. W. Robert Godfrey guides you through the book of Revelation chapter by chapter, clears away confusion, offers practical insight, and equips you for a new and worshipful encounter with the risen and returning King.

This study guide is a companion to the video teaching series. Whether you are using the DVDs, streaming the videos on Ligonier.org, or going through the course in Ligonier Connect, this resource is designed to help you make the most of the learning experience. For each message in the series, there is a corresponding lesson in this guide. Here is what you will find in each lesson:

INTRODUCTION	The introduction is a brief paragraph that summarizes the content covered in the lecture and considered in the study guide lesson. **How to use:** Use the introduction to each lesson to get a sense of the big picture before watching the video. Refer to these statements as you work through the study guide to remind you of what you have already covered and where you are headed.
LEARNING GOALS	The learning goals are the knowledge and skills that the study guide lesson will endeavor to equip you with as you work through the lecture content. **How to use:** Familiarize yourself with the goals of each lesson before engaging its contents. Keeping the overall purpose in mind as you watch each video and reflect on or discuss the questions will help you get the most out of each lesson.
KEY IDEAS	The key ideas are the major points or takeaways from the lecture. **How to use:** Use these ideas to prepare yourself for each lesson and to review previous lessons. They describe specifically the knowledge that each lecture is communicating.

REFLECTION & DISCUSSION QUESTIONS	The questions are the guided reflection and/or discussion component of the lesson that is intended to help you prepare for, process, and organize what you are learning. **How to use:** Reflect on individually or discuss in a group the questions in the order in which they appear in the lesson. The time stamps in the right margin indicate where the answers to questions during the video can be found.
PRAYER	The prayer section offers suggestions for how to close the lesson in prayer with respect to what was taught in the lecture. **How to use:** Consider using each lesson's prayer section as a guide to personal or group prayer. These sections follow the ACTS prayer model, which you can learn more about in R.C. Sproul's Crucial Questions booklet *Does Prayer Change Things?* This helpful guide is available as a free e-book at Ligonier.org.
REVIEW QUIZ	The review quiz is a set of six multiple-choice questions that appears at the end of each lesson. **How to use:** Use each quiz to check your comprehension and memory of the major points covered in each lecture. It will be most beneficial to your learning if you take a lesson's quiz either sometime between lessons or just before you begin the next lesson in the study guide.
ANSWER KEY	The answer key provides explanations for the reflection and discussion questions and answers to the multiple-choice questions in the review quiz. **How to use:** Use the answer key to check your own answers or when you do not know the answer. Note: Do not give in too quickly; struggling for a few moments to recall an answer reinforces it in your mind.

Study Schedules

The following table suggests four plans for working through the *Blessed Hope* video teaching series and this companion study guide. Whether you are going through this series on your own or with a group, these schedules should help you plan your study path.

	Extended 26-Week Plan	Standard 24-Week Plan	Abbreviated 12-Week Plan	Intensive 8-Week Plan
Week	**Lesson**			
1	*	1	1 & 2	1–3
2	1	2	3 & 4	4–6
3	2	3	5 & 6	7–9
4	3	4	7 & 8	10–12
5	4	5	9 & 10	13–15
6	5	6	11 & 12	16–18
7	6	7	13 & 14	19–21
8	7	8	15 & 16	22–24
9	8	9	17 & 18	
10	9	10	19 & 20	
11	10	11	21 & 22	
12	11	12	23 & 24	
13	12	13		
14	13	14		
15	14	15		
16	15	16		
17	16	17		
18	17	18		
19	18	19		

	Extended 26-Week Plan	Standard 24-Week Plan	Abbreviated 12-Week Plan	Intensive 8-Week Plan
Week	**Lesson**			
20	19	20		
21	20	21		
22	21	22		
23	22	23		
24	23	24		
25	24			
26	*			

* For these weeks, rather than completing lessons, spend your time discussing and praying about your learning goals for the study (the first week) and the most valuable takeaways from the study (the last week).

1

A Book of Blessing

INTRODUCTION

Many Christians simply do not know what to do with the book of Revelation. Common approaches to this book include treating it as a code to be cracked, as an inside look into events unfolding around the globe, or as an angry diatribe against contemporary culture. In this lesson, Dr. Godfrey will introduce some helpful ideas and strategies for understanding this book as God has intended. As you begin your journey through Revelation, Dr. Godfrey's hope is that you will be blessed to understand God's Word more fully and to live faithfully for Him.

LEARNING GOALS

When you have finished this lesson, you should be able to:

- Identify some of the benefits of studying the book of Revelation
- Summarize the most common interpretive approaches to Revelation
- Describe how the book of Revelation is structured

KEY IDEAS

- Revelation is given to the church not as a puzzle book or secret code but as a book of blessing for every generation of believers.
- Understanding the structure and setting of Revelation is necessary for understanding its message.
- The heart of the book of Revelation is to reveal Jesus Christ and to draw believers closer to Him.

REFLECTION & DISCUSSION QUESTIONS

Before the Video

What Do You Think?

Take a moment to answer the following questions. They will prepare you for the lecture.

- What first comes to mind when you think about the book of Revelation? What are common perceptions of this book in our culture?

- Have you ever studied eschatology? Why or why not? What do you hope to get out of this teaching series?

Scripture Reading

The revelation of Jesus Christ, which God gave him to show to his servants the things that must soon take place. He made it known by sending his angel to his servant John, who bore witness to the word of God and to the testimony of Jesus Christ, even to all that he saw. Blessed is the one who reads aloud the words of this prophecy, and blessed are those who hear, and who keep what is written in it, for the time is near.

—Revelation 1:1–3

- According to these verses, what is the origin of the book of Revelation? What is its purpose?

During the Video

Answer the following questions while you watch the video. They will guide you through the lecture.

The Significance of the Book of Revelation *0:00–4:01*

- What is the connection between the book of Revelation and blessing?

- How will Dr. Godfrey *not* be approaching Revelation during this teaching series? What will be part of his approach?

Approaches to the Book of Revelation *4:01–12:25*

- What four basic approaches to Revelation does Dr. Godfrey mention? What distinguishes each approach?

- Which of these four approaches to Revelation is Dr. Godfrey going to follow in this teaching series? What books does he mention that also take this approach?

The Structure of the Book of Revelation *12:25–24:10*

- How did Dr. Godfrey's outline of the book of Revelation come about? How is this outline organized?

After the Video

Answer the following questions after you have finished the lecture. They will help you identify and summarize the major points.

- Which of the four approaches to the book of Revelation is most familiar to you? Which of them seems most strange?

  If you are in a group, have the members discuss their familiarity with the different views on Revelation. Which views are represented in your group? Has anyone's approach to Revelation changed over time?

- Does everyone agree on a basic structure or outline for the book of Revelation? Do you think this is helpful or harmful? Explain your answer.

  If you are in a group, have the members each take a few minutes to sketch out a brief outline of Revelation 1:1–3. Compare them. What do they have in common, and how are they different?

- The book of Revelation is the revelation of Jesus Christ—that is, its intent is to make Jesus known to its readers. How has Jesus used Scripture to reveal Himself to you?

  If you are in a group, have some members share specific Bible verses or passages that have shown Christ to them in new or meaningful ways.

PRAYER

Commit what you have learned from God's Word in this lesson to prayer.

- Praise God for providing His church with a book of blessing for every generation.
- Confess any fear, pride, indifference, or other improper attitudes of the heart that you bring with you to this study of Revelation and the end times.
- Thank God for revealing Himself through this mysterious book.
- Ask God to open up your mind and your heart to encounter Jesus anew in this study.

REVIEW QUIZ

Use these multiple-choice questions to measure what you learned from this lesson.

1. The book of Revelation is meant to convey blessing to each generation of Christians.
   a. True
   b. False
2. The preterist approach to Revelation closely associates the book with which of the following years?
   a. 30
   b. 70
   c. 1517
   d. 2012
3. Dispensationalism is a popular form of which of the following interpretive approaches to Revelation?
   a. Church-historical approach
   b. Futurist approach
   c. Present-blessing approach
   d. Preterist approach
4. Why did Dr. Godfrey formulate his own outline of the book of Revelation?
   a. No good outline existed for the book of Revelation.
   b. All outlines of the book of Revelation are outdated.
   c. His outline needed to follow a preterist approach to the book.
   d. His outline needed to follow the fruit of his study of the book.
5. Which of the following does *not* appear in groups of seven in Revelation?
   a. Beasts
   b. Churches
   c. Plagues
   d. Seals

6. Which of the following best describes the original meaning of the word *apocalypse*?
    a. "A cataclysmic disaster"
    b. "A lifting of a veil"
    c. "A return after an extended absence"
    d. "An outpouring of judgment"

Answer Key—A Book of Blessing

REFLECTION & DISCUSSION QUESTIONS

Before the Video

What Do You Think?

These are personal questions. The answers should be based on your own knowledge and experience.

Scripture Reading

- According to these verses, what is the origin of the book of Revelation? What is its purpose?

  Revelation 1:1–3 states that God the Father gave this revelation to Jesus Christ, who in turn made it known to the Apostle John through an angel. God gave this revelation to the servants of Jesus to show them "the things that must soon take place." Other aspects of the purpose of this book are that it would serve as a revelation "of Jesus Christ"—that is, to reveal Christ Himself—and that it might impart blessing to those who read it and put its teaching into practice.

During the Video

The Significance of the Book of Revelation

- What is the connection between the book of Revelation and blessing?

  The opening verses of Revelation declare that those who read the words of this prophecy aloud, those who hear them, and those who keep them are all blessed. Dr. Godfrey expresses his hope that as a result of this study of Revelation, you will be blessed in your understanding of God's Word and in your efforts to live faithfully for Him.

- How will Dr. Godfrey *not* be approaching Revelation during this teaching series? What will be part of his approach?

  In this teaching series, Dr. Godfrey will not be approaching Revelation as a puzzle book, as a code to be cracked, or as a book that is incomprehensible. Instead, he will approach Revelation through the lens of how God is speaking blessing to His people in every generation. This approach will view Revelation as a whole, coherent message.

Approaches to the Book of Revelation

- What four basic approaches to Revelation does Dr. Godfrey mention? What distinguishes each approach?

One interpretive approach to Revelation is the preterist approach, which sees the book as having already been mostly or completely fulfilled by events that took place surrounding the destruction of the temple in AD 70. A second approach to Revelation is the church-historical approach, which sees the book as a prophecy about the whole history of the church, century by century, from the ascension of Christ to His second coming. A third approach is the futurist approach, which views most of Revelation as foretelling future events that have not yet taken place. Finally, Dr. Godfrey mentions a fourth approach that could be called the idealist school, the spiritualist school, or the present-blessing school. This approach views the book as describing what is taking place throughout the history of the church in every generation, culminating in the return of Christ.

- Which of these four approaches to Revelation is Dr. Godfrey going to follow in this teaching series? What books does he mention that also take this approach?

  Dr. Godfrey will follow the fourth approach, which he describes as the present-blessing school, in this teaching series. Other examples of this approach in Reformed scholarship include William Hendriksen's More than Conquerors, *G.K. Beale's* The Book of Revelation, *and Dennis Johnson's* Triumph of the Lamb.

The Structure of the Book of Revelation

- How did Dr. Godfrey's outline of the book of Revelation come about? How is this outline organized?

  In his study of Revelation, Dr. Godfrey paid careful attention to how the book presents itself and kept noticing the recurring pattern of sevens throughout the book. The more he noticed this theme, the more he began to suspect that this theme of seven is the controlling structure of the book. As a result, he will be arguing in this teaching series that Revelation consists of seven major cycles, each with seven subpoints.

After the Video

- Which of the four approaches to the book of Revelation is most familiar to you? Which of them seems most strange?

  The answer to this question should name one of the four main interpretive approaches (preterist, church-historical, futurist, or present-blessing) that you have interacted with the most and one of the four views that you find, or have found, particularly difficult to embrace or understand. In your answer, there should be a definition of this approach based on the lecture.

- Does everyone agree on a basic structure or outline for the book of Revelation? Do you think this is helpful or harmful? Explain your answer.

  Dr. Godfrey shared how he approached his friend Dr. Dennis Johnson to ask if it was appropriate for him to come up with his own outline of Revelation. Dr. Johnson replied, "Everybody has their own outline of the book of Revelation. Why shouldn't you be able to have yours?" One benefit of this plurality of outlines is that it shows a commitment on the part of many believers to studying this book for themselves and forming their own conclusions. In his efforts to outline this book, Dr. Godfrey was careful to let Revelation speak for itself rather than imposing a man-made structure on it.

- The book of Revelation is the revelation of Jesus Christ. What should you then anticipate in this study on Revelation?

  Because the book of Revelation is "the revelation of Jesus Christ" (1:1), you should anticipate gaining a fuller picture of who Jesus is through studying it. The book of Revelation is the revelation from Jesus about Jesus. It is the testimony of Jesus Christ, and it speaks directly to His church.

REVIEW QUIZ

Lesson 1

1. **A.**
   Dr. Godfrey explained that his approach to Revelation in this teaching series will focus on how God is speaking through this book to His people in every generation to impart spiritual blessing to them.

2. **B.**
   Preterism, which considers most or all of the book of Revelation to have been fulfilled in the past, associates much of this book's content with the destruction of the Jewish temple in AD 70.

3. **B.**
   Dispensationalism is an influential and well-known example of the futurist approach to Revelation. From its nineteenth-century origins, it has spread quickly to become the most common approach to Revelation in the United States today.

4. **D.**
   Dr. Godfrey was encouraged to form his own outline of Revelation because of the abundance of outlines that already existed for the book of Revelation. Dr. Godfrey had reached different conclusions about the structure of the book in his study, so he needed to remain true to his study of the book.

5. **A.**
   The controlling structure of Revelation comprises sets of seven. In addition to the structure of seven cycles, other sets of seven in this book include seven letters to seven churches, seven seals, seven trumpets, and seven plagues. The beasts of Revelation, which appear later in the book, are an exception to the theme of sevens.

6. **B.**
   The Greek word apokalypsis, *from which we get our English word* apocalypse, *refers to the act of lifting or drawing back a veil so that what was once concealed may now be seen and understood.*

2

Time, Cycles, & Symbols

INTRODUCTION

The book of Revelation is not just a book of abstract predictions about a distant future. Instead, it tackles real and practical challenges that all generations of believers face. In the opening chapter of this book, John wastes no time in addressing the suffering and adversity that he and his fellow Christians have experienced. Yet, in the midst of trials and tribulation, he expresses a vision of God's redemptive mission that offers hope to God's people in all eras.

LEARNING GOALS

When you have finished this lesson, you should be able to:

- Understand some key principles of interpreting biblical prophecy
- Identify the presence of each person of the Trinity in Revelation 1
- Articulate a theology of hope through suffering that is rooted in the structure of Revelation

KEY IDEAS

- Christians can profit from reading Revelation because it addresses immediate realities in the life of faith.
- Christians can persevere and find hope in times of suffering, knowing that God is with them and will deliver them from their trials and tribulations.
- Christians can live with joy, knowing that the reality of heaven is just over our shoulders if we have the eyes of faith to see it.

REFLECTION & DISCUSSION QUESTIONS

Before the Video

What Do You Think?

Take a moment to answer the following questions. They will prepare you for the lecture.

- How would you define prophecy? What would you say is the purpose of prophecy in the Bible?

- Is it appropriate to interpret parts of the Bible as symbolic? How do we know when to interpret the Bible symbolically and when to interpret it more literally?

Scripture Reading

John to the seven churches that are in Asia: Grace to you and peace from him who is and who was and who is to come, and from the seven spirits who are before his throne, and from Jesus Christ the faithful witness, the firstborn of the dead, and the ruler of kings on earth. To him who loves us and has freed us from our sins by his blood and made us a kingdom, priests to his God and Father, to him be glory and dominion forever and ever. Amen. Behold, he is coming with the clouds, and every eye will see him, even those who pierced him, and all tribes of the earth will wail on account of him. Even so. Amen. "I am the Alpha and the Omega," says the Lord God, "who is and who was and who is to come, the Almighty."

—Revelation 1:4–8

- The book of Revelation is a revelation of Jesus Christ. What does this passage reveal about Jesus? What does this passage reveal about those who believe in Him?

During the Video

Answer the following questions while you watch the video. They will guide you through the lecture.

Important Themes of Revelation *0:00–11:13*

- How should believers interpret Revelation's claim that these things must take place soon?

- What role does the theme of overcoming and conquering play in Revelation?

John's Introduction *11:13–26:39*

- What does the reference to seven spirits in verse 4 refer to? Why is the number seven used?

- Revelation 1:9 mentions both the tribulation and the kingdom. How does Dr. Godfrey explain the relationship between these two realities?

After the Video

Answer the following questions after you have finished the lecture. They will help you identify and summarize the major points.

- How do the cycles of Revelation present the theme of suffering? What does this teach about the role of suffering in the Christian life?

  If you are in a group, have the members share examples of a time that they persevered through suffering.

- What do these opening verses of Revelation say about who runs the world today? How is this message from Revelation good news to you?

  If you are in a group, have the members identify worldly powers that appear to be in charge. How does God demonstrate His sovereignty over all people, nations, and things?

- How would you describe John's circumstances at the time when he suddenly had this vision of the heavenly temple? In what life circumstances have you most powerfully experienced God's presence?

  If you are in a group, have the members reflect on moments and factors in their lives that God has used to draw them into His presence.

PRAYER

Commit what you have learned from God's Word in this lesson to prayer.

- Praise God for establishing His kingdom even amid present trials and tribulations.

- Confess any doubt or fear that you are wrestling with right now.
- Thank the Father, Son, and Holy Spirit for the unique ways that each of them blesses you.
- Ask God to help you be more than a conqueror in the midst of your present challenges.

REVIEW QUIZ

Use these multiple-choice questions to measure what you learned from this lesson.

1. Which of the following best describes the role of prophecy throughout Scripture?
   a. A code to interpret major events
   b. Descriptions of the end of time
   c. Pastoral instruction for the here and now
   d. Words about the future

2. What main purpose of God still needs to be accomplished before Christ's second coming?
   a. The Christianization of society
   b. The gathering of the elect
   c. The punishing of evildoers
   d. The rebuilding of a physical temple

3. Revelation describes suffering experienced by both the righteous and the wicked.
   a. True
   b. False

4. John wrote the book of Revelation to churches located in which modern-day country?
   a. Greece
   b. Israel
   c. Syria
   d. Turkey

5. The claim that certain elements of Revelation are symbolic undermines a literal interpretation of Scripture.
   a. True
   b. False

6. Which of the following best describes the relationship between tribulation and the kingdom?
   a. Believers are spared tribulation, and they experience the kingdom only.
   b. Believers experience tribulation before they experience the kingdom.
   c. Believers experience tribulation after they experience the kingdom.
   d. Believers experience tribulation and the kingdom at the same time.

Answer Key—Time, Cycles, & Symbols

REFLECTION & DISCUSSION QUESTIONS

Before the Video

What Do You Think?

These are personal questions. The answers should be based on your own knowledge and experience.

Scripture Reading

- The book of Revelation is a revelation of Jesus Christ. What does this passage reveal about Jesus? What does this passage reveal about those who believe in Him?

  This passage describes Jesus as "the faithful witness," "the firstborn of the dead," and "the ruler of kings on earth." It also recounts His redemptive work on the cross and declares that He is coming again. In describing Christ's work of redemption, this passage proclaims that believers are loved by Jesus, have been freed from their sins, and have now become a kingdom of priests in His service. In describing Jesus as the firstborn of the dead, this passage also indicates that we, too, will one day be raised from the dead.

During the Video

Important Themes of Revelation

- How should believers interpret Revelation's claim that these things must take place soon?

  The book of Revelation is bookended by statements declaring that these things must take place soon. This verbiage shows us that the content of this book applies to believers now, not just two thousand years ago or in the distant future. This wording is also rooted in the fact that Jesus' work on the cross is finished; there is nothing else that needs to be accomplished redemptively before the second coming except for the gathering of God's elect. Therefore, we are to view the events of Revelation with a sense of immediacy, knowing that this book describes the present age in which we live.

- What role does the theme of overcoming and conquering play in Revelation?

  This book, particularly in the letters to the seven churches, urges believers to overcome. This exhortation reiterates Jesus' statement in John 16:33 that He has "overcome the world" and reflects Paul's declaration in Romans 8:37 that believers are "more than conquerors" in Christ Jesus. In the face of the Roman Empire's apparent conquest of the known world, this motif reminded first-century believers that Jesus was the true conqueror. John wants his readers to live confidently, knowing that our victory is certain in Christ.

John's Introduction

- What does the reference to seven spirits in verse 4 refer to? Why is the number seven used?

  Revelation 1:4–5 contains a Trinitarian blessing given to the church. The seven spirits before the throne mentioned in verse 4 refer not to seven separate spirits but to the Holy Spirit. The number seven is used to express the completion and perfection of the Spirit's character and His ministry to the church.

- Revelation 1:9 mentions both the tribulation and the kingdom. How does Dr. Godfrey explain the relationship between these two realities?

  John introduces himself as a partner to the churches in the tribulation and the kingdom. Although many interpreters of Revelation have separated these two realities into a period of tribulation followed by a subsequent manifestation of the kingdom, the text makes it clear that these two realities are linked. Believers currently live in an eschatological age in which the arrival of God's kingdom overlaps with continued human sin and suffering until Christ's return. Consequently, we experience tribulation and the kingdom at the same time until the kingdom is finally consummated at the second coming of Jesus.

After the Video

- How do the cycles of Revelation present the theme of suffering? What does this teach about the role of suffering in the Christian life?

  Dr. Godfrey points out that the first three cycles in Revelation offer encouragement to the church in the midst of suffering. Furthermore, the central cycle in the book is about the church persevering through suffering. Finally, the last three cycles speak of deliverance from suffering. The message that emerges from these cycles is one of the church being faithful to endure suffering and hardship, knowing that it will not go on forever.

- What do these opening verses of Revelation say about who runs the world today? How is this message from Revelation good news to you?

  Revelation 1:5 describes Jesus as "the ruler of kings on earth," indicating His sovereign control over even the most powerful human figures and institutions. To the early church, this message offered hope that even though Caesar appeared to be in control, God's kingdom was greater still. Believers today can draw hope from this passage in a variety of ways.

- How would you describe John's circumstances at the time when he suddenly had this vision of the heavenly temple? In what life circumstances have you most powerfully experienced God's presence?

John's exile on Patmos was a season of ministry characterized by suffering and patient endurance. In the midst of his ordinary celebration of the Lord's Day, he experienced a glorious vision of the heavenly temple. Many believers today also encounter Christ in the midst of ordinary, challenging, or disappointing seasons of life. Answers to the second question will vary from person to person.

REVIEW QUIZ

Lesson 2

1. **C.**
   Dr. Godfrey points out that the primary purpose of prophecy throughout the Bible is not to predict the future or to reveal distant events. Rather, prophecy is to be understood as God's Word to help and direct His people pastorally in the present.

2. **B.**
   The New Testament's approach to eschatological time is rooted in the reality that Jesus' work on the cross is finished. Nothing else needs to happen redemptively before the second coming except for the gathering of God's elect from every nation, tribe, and tongue.

3. **A.**
   Rather than focusing exclusively on the suffering of the righteous, Revelation—particularly in the third cycle—also describes the suffering of the wicked.

4. **D.**
   In Revelation 1:11, John receives instructions to write this book to churches in the cities of Ephesus, Smyrna, Pergamum, Thyatira, Sardis, Philadelphia, and Laodicea. All of these cities were located in a relatively small geographic area in what is now the modern nation of Turkey.

5. **B.**
   Recognition of symbolic language in Scripture does not conflict with a literal reading of God's Word. To read the Bible literally is to read it as its authors intended. To insist on a wooden, word-for-word interpretation when an author intended a symbolic interpretation is actually to fail to interpret the Bible literally.

6. **D.**
   In Revelation 1:9, John describes himself as a partner with the other believers in both their tribulations and the kingdom. This verse openly expresses a truth that is demonstrated throughout the rest of this book: tribulation and the kingdom exist side by side until the day when Christ returns to consummate His kingdom.

3

Understanding the Seven Letters

INTRODUCTION

The first chapter of Revelation concludes with a stunning heavenly scene. Jesus, the risen and glorious Conqueror, stands in majesty in the midst of His churches. Even though a glimpse of Jesus in glory is enough to bring John to his knees, Jesus speaks gentle words of blessing to His people. As we begin to explore Christ's letters to the seven churches, we will behold a picture not just of Jesus' sovereign majesty but also of His tender, pastoral heart for His people.

LEARNING GOALS

When you have finished this lesson, you should be able to:

- Describe Jesus' heavenly appearance and His care for His church
- Identify common features and themes of the letters to the seven churches
- Name four spiritual adversaries of the early church and their equivalents today

KEY IDEAS

- Jesus rules in the heavenly temple and is worthy of all praise.
- Jesus is deeply committed to His church and watches over individual churches with care.
- Jesus speaks words of blessing to His people and exhorts them to live faithfully for Him.

REFLECTION & DISCUSSION QUESTIONS

Before the Video

What Do You Think?

Take a moment to answer the following questions. They will prepare you for the lecture.

- What comes to mind when you imagine Jesus? Which of His attributes are most obvious as you envision Him?

- What is the most memorable letter that you have received? Who sent it to you? How did its message affect you?

Scripture Reading

Then I turned to see the voice that was speaking to me, and on turning I saw seven golden lampstands, and in the midst of the lampstands one like a son of man, clothed with a long robe and with a golden sash around his chest. The hairs of his head were white, like white wool, like snow. His eyes were like a flame of fire, his feet were like burnished bronze, refined in a furnace, and his voice was like the roar of many waters. In his right hand he held seven stars, from his mouth came a sharp two-edged sword, and his face was like the sun shining in full strength. When I saw him, I fell at his feet as though dead. But he laid his right hand on me, saying, "Fear not, I am the first and the last, and the living one. I died, and behold I am alive forevermore, and I have the keys of Death and Hades. Write therefore the things that you have seen, those that are and those that are to take place after this. As for the mystery of the seven stars that you saw in my right hand, and the seven golden lampstands, the seven stars are the angels of the seven churches, and the seven lampstands are the seven churches."

—Revelation 1:12–20

- How does Jesus describe Himself in this passage? How do these verses present the relationship between Jesus and His church?

During the Video

Answer the following questions while you watch the video. They will guide you through the lecture.

The Temple and the Son of Man *0:00–14:23*

- How does the account of Elisha in 2 Kings 6:15–17 illustrate a major theme of Revelation?

- Is the description of Jesus in Revelation 1:12–16 literal or symbolic? What do some of these specific details mean?

Characteristics of the Seven Letters *14:23–24:18*

- What seven elements are present in each of the letters to the seven churches?

- Which four enemies of the church appear in the seven letters?

After the Video

Answer the following questions after you have finished the lecture. They will help you identify and summarize the major points.

- What are the seven blessings of the book of Revelation that Dr. Godfrey mentioned? How do they offer hope to Christians today?

  If you are in a group, have the members read these blessings (Revelation 1:3; 14:13; 16:15; 19:9; 20:6; 22:7; and 22:14) together and discuss them. Which are most encouraging? Which are most challenging?
- How can Christians today profit from reading letters that were written to address particular problems that churches were facing two thousand years ago?

  If you are in a group, have the members identify similarities and differences between the challenges these seven ancient churches faced and those that your own churches face today.
- Imagine that Jesus was writing a letter to your congregation. What are some things He might praise in your church? What accusations might He bring against your church?

  If you are in a group, have the members discuss how they think Jesus might assess their own congregations. Take a few minutes to pray for your churches together.

PRAYER

Commit what you have learned from God's Word in this lesson to prayer.

- Praise Christ for His holiness, majesty, and sovereign rule over all things.

- Confess areas of your life where you struggle to live faithfully for Christ.
- Thank God for His care over your local church.
- Ask God to help you and your church overcome all hardship, temptation, and adversity.

REVIEW QUIZ

Use these multiple-choice questions to measure what you learned from this lesson.

1. What did a lampstand represent to a pious first-century Jewish mind?
   a. The light of God's favor on His chosen people
   b. The presence of God among His people
   c. The righteous deeds of the saints in a dark world
   d. The searing fire of divine judgment
2. Where in the Bible is the most detailed physical description of Jesus found?
   a. Isaiah 53
   b. Matthew 17
   c. Revelation 1
   d. Revelation 19
3. Which of the following does *not* appear in Christ's letters to the seven churches?
   a. An exhortation to live faithfully
   b. An identification of Christ
   c. A promise to those who overcome
   d. A summary of the gospel
4. The Christian understanding that Jesus is the Messiah is based on which of the following?
   a. An Apostolic reading of the Old Testament
   b. A Hellenistic reading of the Old Testament
   c. A prophetic reading of the Old Testament
   d. A rabbinic reading of the Old Testament
5. Which of the following is *not* identified as an enemy of the church in the seven letters?
   a. Civil government
   b. False teachers
   c. Pagan religion
   d. Unbelieving neighbors
6. The letters to the churches recognize a distinction between faithful members and unfaithful members of the church.
   a. True
   b. False

Answer Key— Understanding the Seven Letters

REFLECTION & DISCUSSION QUESTIONS

Before the Video

What Do You Think?

These are personal questions. The answers should be based on your own knowledge and experience.

Scripture Reading

- How does Jesus describe Himself in this passage? How do these verses present the relationship between Jesus and His church?

  Jesus describes Himself in terms that communicate His divinity, eternality, redemptive work on the cross, and victory over sin and death. These verses describe Him in the midst of His churches, holding the power of the spirits of those churches in His hand. This expresses His nearness to His people and His sovereign oversight of His church.

During the Video

The Temple and the Son of Man

- How does the account of Elisha in 2 Kings 6:15–17 illustrate a major theme of Revelation?

  In 2 Kings 6, a vast Syrian army had surrounded the city where Elisha and his servant were staying. Because his servant was frightened by the might of the Syrians, Elisha asked God to open the servant's eyes to behold the even greater heavenly army that surrounded the Syrians. This account illustrates the principle of seeing with eyes of faith what a merely human eye cannot perceive. This is a significant theme of Revelation, which invites believers to see beyond the might of earthly empires to behold by faith the victorious and matchless power of Christ.

- Is the description of Jesus in Revelation 1:12–16 literal or symbolic? What do some of these specific details mean?

  This description is meant to be understood in terms of the rich symbolism that appears in these verses. The overall picture presented in these verses is of the power and purity of Christ. The two-edged sword coming from His mouth represents the determinative power of His words when they come in judgment. The white color of His hair links Him to the eternal God, the Ancient of Days. The seven stars and lampstands describe His nearness to His people and His sovereign care for them.

Characteristics of the Seven Letters

- What seven elements are present in each of the letters to the seven churches?

  (1) Christ commands John to write each letter; (2) Christ identifies Himself at the beginning of each letter; (3) Christ praises the good works of all but two churches; (4) Christ brings accusations of sin against all but two churches; (5) Christ issues a call to repentance or words of encouragement; (6) Christ exhorts the churches how to live; and (7) Christ concludes with a promise to those who overcome.

- Which four enemies of the church appear in the seven letters?

  (1) Rome, representing oppressive civil government; (2) the leaders of the synagogues of unbelief who oppose the Apostolic understanding that Jesus is the Messiah of the Old Testament; (3) pagan religion, which was often integral to the cultures and local economies of the cities where Christians lived; and (4) false teachers who profess to be Christians and threaten the church from within.

After the Video

- What are the seven blessings of the book of Revelation that Dr. Godfrey mentioned? How do they offer hope to Christians today?

  The following blessings from Revelation offer hope to Christians of all generations who place their trust in Christ. These blessings are extended to believers by virtue of their union with Christ. Some of them also offer guidance and exhortation to persevere in faithfulness in the midst of suffering and hardship.

  - *"Blessed is the one who reads aloud the words of this prophecy, and blessed are those who hear, and who keep what is written in it, for the time is near" (1:3).*
  - *"'Blessed are the dead who die in the Lord from now on.' 'Blessed indeed,' says the Spirit, 'that they may rest from their labors, for their deeds follow after them!'" (14:13).*
  - *"Blessed is the one who stays awake, keeping his garments on, that he may not go about naked and be seen exposed!" (16:15).*
  - *"Blessed are those who are invited to the marriage supper of the Lamb" (19:9).*
  - *"Blessed and holy is the one who shares in the first resurrection! Over such the second death has no power, but they will be priests of God and of Christ, and they will reign with him for a thousand years" (20:6).*
  - *"Blessed is the one who keeps the words of the prophecy of this book" (22:7).*
  - *"Blessed are those who wash their robes, so that they may have the right to the tree of life and that they may enter the city by the gates" (22:14).*

- How can Christians today profit from reading letters that were written to address particular problems that churches were facing two thousand years ago?

  Dr. Godfrey points out that these letters can remind us that not every church has the same problems. By studying these different problems, we can be encouraged and better informed to serve God faithfully in our own contexts. We can profit from the good and bad examples of other churches and use their struggles as a template for self-assessment.

- Imagine that Jesus was writing a letter to your congregation. What are some things He might praise in your church? What accusations might He bring against your church?

  Answers to this question will vary from person to person. Answers should draw from the lecture and include a balanced assessment of areas of strength and needed growth.

REVIEW QUIZ

Lesson 3

1. **B.**
   Pious first-century Jews would have associated the lampstands in Revelation 1 with the lampstand in the temple, which represented the presence of God among His people.

2. **C.**
   The symbolic description of Jesus in the heavenly temple found in Revelation 1:12–16 is the longest and most detailed summary of Jesus' appearance found anywhere in Scripture. Yet, this description is composed of symbols that communicate His majesty and divine attributes rather than His physical features.

3. **D.**
   Among the standard features of the seven letters are Christ's identification of Himself at the beginning of each letter, an exhortation to the churches on how to live, and a promise to those who overcome. Though the gospel is presupposed and implied in these letters, it is not explicitly summarized.

4. **A.**
   The divergence between the Jewish and Christian faiths is based in their different understandings of the Jewish Messiah. Christianity is rooted in an Apostolic reading of the Old Testament, which recognizes Jesus as the Messiah. Contemporary Judaism is rooted in a rabbinic reading of the Old Testament, which does not recognize Jesus as the Messiah.

5. **D.**
   The letters to the churches identify civil governments, leaders of the synagogues of unbelief, pagan religion, and false teachers as enemies of the church. Scripture makes it clear that the Christian's struggle is not against unbelieving people but rather against "the authorities, against the cosmic powers over this present darkness, against the spiritual forces of evil in the heavenly places" (Eph. 6:12). These spiritual foes are linked to the enemies listed in the seven letters.

6. **A.**
   These letters demonstrate an awareness of the differences among members of the visible churches to whom they are addressed. These letters recognize that there can be faithful individuals in an unfaithful church and vice versa.

4

Letters to Ephesus & Smyrna

INTRODUCTION

After beholding the glorious vision of Jesus in the heavenly temple, John was commanded to record letters from Jesus to seven specific churches. In this lecture, Dr. Godfrey explores the first two letters, which deal with very different circumstances. Even though these letters were written two thousand years ago, they still have much to teach believers today.

LEARNING GOALS

When you have finished this lesson, you should be able to:

- Describe the literary structure and features of the letters to the seven churches
- Summarize the key messages of the letters to the churches in Ephesus and Smyrna

KEY IDEAS

- The structure of the seven letters reveals Christ's pastoral care for His people and His intimate knowledge of what they need.
- Sound doctrine and righteous living matter little without love for Jesus Christ.
- Even when believers suffer to the point of physical death, they have no need to fear "the second death" because they belong to Christ.

REFLECTION & DISCUSSION QUESTIONS

Before the Video

What Do You Think?

Take a moment to answer the following questions. They will prepare you for the lecture.

- What does love for Jesus look like in the practical, day-to-day life of a Christian?

- Describe the cost of following Jesus. What are some sacrifices and difficulties that you have experienced for the sake of Christ?

Scripture Reading

> *"I know your tribulation and your poverty (but you are rich) and the slander of those who say that they are Jews and are not, but are a synagogue of Satan. Do not fear what you are about to suffer. Behold, the devil is about to throw some of you into prison, that you may be tested, and for ten days you will have tribulation. Be faithful unto death, and I will give you the crown of life."*
>
> —Revelation 2:9–10

- What hardships are described in these verses? What reassurance does Jesus offer His people who are experiencing these hardships?

During the Video

Answer the following questions while you watch the video. They will guide you through the lecture.

Literary and Historical Features *0:00–8:43*

- What is a chiasm? Where does this name come from?

- Where were Ephesus and Smyrna situated in relation to John's location on Patmos?

The Letter to Ephesus *8:43–14:52*

- Why did the Ephesians face the possibility of having their lampstand removed?

- Who were the Nicolaitans? What can we learn from this?

The Letter to Smyrna *14:52–24:10*

- Is the letter to the church in Smyrna anti-Semitic? Why or why not?

- To what reality does the "second death" in the letter to Smyrna refer?

After the Video

Answer the following questions after you have finished the lecture. They will help you identify and summarize the major points.

- How does the order of the seven letters reveal a specific literary structure? How does it reveal a geographic pattern?

  If you are in a group, have the members discuss and share examples of how the order in which things are arranged can affect their meaning.

- What was the first love that the Ephesians had abandoned? In what way had they abandoned it? How can Christians today learn from this warning?

  If you are in a group, have the members identify things that tend to distract them from Jesus.

- What does the letter to Smyrna teach believers about suffering and faithfulness?

  If you are in a group, have the members share an example of faithfulness in the midst of suffering that they find encouraging.

PRAYER

Commit what you have learned from God's Word in this lesson to prayer.

- Praise God for providing guidance and care to His people in ancient times and today.
- Confess specific distractions in your life that divert your attention away from Christ.
- Thank God for giving you strength to overcome difficulties and hardships.
- Ask God to help you love and follow Jesus more joyfully and faithfully.

REVIEW QUIZ

Use these multiple-choice questions to measure what you learned from this lesson.

1. In the literary arrangement of the seven letters, which churches are in the center of the chiasm?
   a. Churches receiving a call to persevere
   b. Churches receiving a mixture of rebuke and praise
   c. Churches receiving glowing commendations
   d. Churches receiving severe warnings

2. Which of the seven cities was located closest to John's place of exile?
    a. Ephesus
    b. Laodicea
    c. Pergamum
    d. Smyrna
3. Which group were the Ephesians commended for opposing?
    a. Judaizers
    b. Marcionites
    c. Nicolaitans
    d. Roman imperial cult
4. The letter to Ephesus is best summarized as which of the following?
    a. Letter of faith
    b. Letter of hope
    c. Letter of life
    d. Letter of love
5. The letter to Smyrna is best summarized as which of the following?
    a. Letter of hope
    b. Letter of life
    c. Letter of love
    d. Letter of peace
6. *Synagogue* is a Hebrew word that means "the gathering together."
    a. True
    b. False

Answer Key—Letters to Ephesus & Smyrna

REFLECTION & DISCUSSION QUESTIONS

Before the Video

What Do You Think?

These are personal questions. The answers should be based on your own knowledge and experience.

Scripture Reading

- What hardships are described in these verses? What reassurance does Jesus offer His people who are experiencing these hardships?

  The believers in Smyrna are described as having endured tribulation, poverty, and slander. Moreover, they are told that they will experience future suffering, imprisonment, and the prospect of death. Nevertheless, Jesus tells them not to be afraid, affirms that they are spiritually rich despite their material poverty, and promises the crown of life to those who remain faithful.

During the Video

Literary and Historical Features

- What is a chiasm? Where does this name come from?

  A chiasm is a literary feature that derives its name from the Greek letter chi, *which resembles an X. It is so called because it involves sequences of parallel elements that bookend a central concept. Another way of describing this literary feature is as a thematic pyramid that goes up one side, includes a central point at the top, and then goes down in a parallel way on the other side.*

- Where were Ephesus and Smyrna situated in relation to John's location on Patmos?

  Patmos, John's place of exile, is located approximately thirty-five miles off the coast of modern Turkey. Ephesus, located near the coast northeast of Patmos, would have been the closest of the seven churches to John's location. Smyrna, also situated on the coast, was located about seventy miles north of Ephesus.

The Letter to Ephesus

- Why did the Ephesians face the possibility of having their lampstand removed?

  Jesus accused the Ephesian church of abandoning the love for Him that it had at first. In this letter, He calls the Ephesians to repent of this neglect lest their lampstand be removed. In other words, He is warning them that if they lost sight of

Christ as the center of their faith, the identity and future of their worshiping community would also be lost.

- Who were the Nicolaitans? What can we learn from this?

  The only references to the Nicolaitans appear in the letters to Ephesus and Pergamum in Revelation 2. Extrabiblical sources do not provide a clear record of who these people were. In short, we have no idea who the Nicolaitans were or why they were so dangerous to these churches. This reality reminds us to be humbly aware that we don't understand every single detail in the Bible, and it shows us that we do not have to know every detail of the biblical text for it to be able to speak to us.

The Letter to Smyrna

- Is the letter to the church in Smyrna anti-Semitic? Why or why not?

  Anti-Semitism, like all forms of racism and prejudice, is an evil that Christians must oppose. Although critics may label Revelation 2:9 as anti-Semitic, it actually denounces those who falsely claim to be Jews. Biblical Christianity, as the heir of the Jewish faith, is in fact decidedly pro-Semitic.

- To what reality does the "second death" in the letter to Smyrna refer?

  The "second death" mentioned in Revelation 2:11 refers to the outcome of the final judgment in which those whose names are not written in the book of life are cast into the lake of fire (Rev. 20:14; 21:8). Christians may fear the first death, but the death that is truly to be feared is the second death, which believers will never experience.

After the Video

- How does the order of the seven letters reveal a specific literary structure? How does it reveal a geographic pattern?

  The seven letters to the churches are arranged chiastically. The first and seventh letters are critical letters in which the churches are threatened with having their lampstand removed. Next, the second and sixth letters are to churches that are commended for their faithfulness. Finally, the three central letters contain a blend of rebuke and commendation. The letters are arranged both literarily and geographically. Their order in Revelation reflects the order in which a courier would travel to each of the cities, forming an arc through western Turkey.

- What was the first love that the Ephesians had abandoned? In what way had they abandoned it? How can Christians today learn from this warning?

  The first love of the Ephesians was Jesus' love for them and their love for Jesus. Though Christ commends them for their sound doctrine and faithful obedience, this warning indicates that sound doctrine and right behavior are not enough if we have lost our focus on Christ. This warning reminds Christians today that orthodoxy and obedience matter little if we do not have an affectionate love for Christ.

- What does the letter to Smyrna teach believers about suffering and faithfulness?

  This letter speaks openly about the resistance and persecution that the believers in Smyrna were experiencing. It tells them that they would even experience imprisonment for ten days—likely symbolic for a time that seems long but that God has limited. Yet, it also offers them encouragement that God knows their sufferings, affirmation that they are the true people of God, and hope that their faithfulness will be rewarded with the victor's crown.

REVIEW QUIZ

Lesson 4

1. **B.**
   The churches whose letters appear at the center of the chiastic literary order are churches that were neither solely praised or critiqued but that received a mixture of rebuke and commendation.

2. **A.**
   Ephesus, located on the Turkish coast thirty-five miles northeast of Patmos, was the closest of the seven cities to John's place of exile.

3. **C.**
   In the letter to the church at Ephesus, Jesus commends the Ephesian believers for opposing the Nicolaitans. Although very little is known today about this group, the Nicolaitans are mentioned in two of the letters to the seven churches.

4. **D.**
   Dr. Godfrey describes the letter to Ephesus as a letter of love, one that called the Ephesian believers to return to their first love for Jesus Christ by remembering their love, repenting, and returning to the works they were doing from the start.

5. **B.**
   Dr. Godfrey describes the letter to Smyrna as a letter of life, one that promised life to the faithful, enduring, persecuted, and suffering Christians of Smyrna. Jesus promises that "the one who conquers will not be hurt by the second death" (Rev. 2:11b).

6. **B.**
   Even though the word synagogue *refers to a Jewish worship gathering, it comes from the Greek language instead of Hebrew. It derives from the Greek verb* synagō, *which means "to gather together."*

5

Letters to Pergamum, Thyatira, & Sardis

INTRODUCTION

Continuing our study of Christ's letters to the seven churches, we will turn our attention in this lecture to the three churches in the center of this literary section. These three congregations—located in the cities of Pergamum, Thyatira, and Sardis—are all commended for their acts of faithfulness to Christ yet still struggle with real problems. To believers of all ages who wrestle with the tension between their desire to live for Christ and their sin, these letters offer both deep encouragement and a call to renewed obedience.

LEARNING GOALS

When you have finished this lesson, you should be able to:

- Summarize the key messages of the letters to the churches in Pergamum, Thyatira, and Sardis
- Explain the significance of the rich imagery used in the three central letters

KEY IDEAS

- The body of Christ includes vivid examples of both fallenness and faithfulness.
- In spite of daily struggles, God will vindicate His people and declare their innocence.
- Christians can take heart that their names are written in the book of life and will never be blotted out.

REFLECTION & DISCUSSION QUESTIONS

Before the Video

What Do You Think?

Take a moment to answer the following questions. They will prepare you for the lecture.

- When have you seen the church at its best? When have you seen it at its worst?

- What aspect of your personal spiritual growth do you most feel good about? In what area do you most desire to grow?

Scripture Reading

"Yet you have still a few names in Sardis, people who have not soiled their garments, and they will walk with me in white, for they are worthy. The one who conquers will be clothed thus in white garments, and I will never blot his name out of the book of life. I will confess his name before my Father and before his angels."

—Revelation 3:4–5

- What metaphor is used to describe those who conquer? What reward is promised to them?

During the Video

Answer the following questions while you watch the video. They will guide you through the lecture.

The Letter to Pergamum — *0:00–7:13*

- What are the references to "Satan's throne" and the place "where Satan dwells" in Revelation 2:13 most likely describing?

- How should we understand the references to Balaam and Balak in Revelation 2:14?

The Letter to Thyatira — *7:13–18:49*

- What is the significance of the reference to Jezebel in Revelation 2:20–23?

- Why is Jesus described as having feet "like burnished bronze" in Revelation 2:18?

The Letter to Sardis *18:49–24:11*

- What is the significance of the white garments in Revelation 3:4–5?

- What does the letter to Sardis say about the book of life?

After the Video

Answer the following questions after you have finished the lecture. They will help you identify and summarize the major points.

- What can we learn from the fact that the three central letters in Revelation are written to churches that are partly commended and partly rebuked? How does this inform our perspective on the body of Christ?

  If you are in a group, have the members discuss what they find encouraging and what they find challenging in these letters.
- In what way is the white stone mentioned in the letter to the church at Pergamum a symbol of life in Christ?

  If you are in a group, have the members describe how they felt when they first became aware that God has declared them to be righteous and innocent in Christ.
- What do the references to Balaam and the morning star in Revelation 2 reveal about God's sovereignty and sense of humor?

  If you are in a group, have the members share an example of a time when they witnessed God's sovereignty and a time when they were reminded that God has a sense of humor.

PRAYER

Commit what you have learned from God's Word in this lesson to prayer.

- Praise God for revealing His sovereignty and humor in Scripture and human experience.
- Confess areas where you have been indifferent to holiness and prone to temptation.

- Thank God for declaring you innocent and for clothing you in Christ's righteousness.
- Ask God to increase your confidence in Christ and desire to live for Him.

REVIEW QUIZ

Use these multiple-choice questions to measure what you learned from this lesson.

1. For what is Antipas remembered in the letter to the church in Pergamum?
   a. Eating food sacrificed to idols
   b. Dying for his faith
   c. Spreading false teaching
   d. Wearing white garments

2. Which of the following was *not* a feature of the ancient city of Pergamum?
   a. Coastal setting
   b. Persecution and martyrdom of Christians
   c. Roman governing presence
   d. Temple to Zeus

3. The letter to Pergamum is best summarized as which of the following?
   a. Letter about holiness
   b. Letter about judgment
   c. Letter about love
   d. Letter about peace

4. The letter to Thyatira is best summarized as which of the following?
   a. Letter about judgment
   b. Letter about life
   c. Letter about searching
   d. Letter about peace

5. Jesus mentions which Old Testament figure by name in the letter to Thyatira?
   a. Ahab
   b. Balaam
   c. Balak
   d. Jezebel

6. The letter to Sardis is best summarized as which of the following?
   a. Letter about holiness
   b. Letter about joy
   c. Letter about judgment
   d. Letter about searching

Answer Key—
Letters to Pergamum, Thyatira, & Sardis

REFLECTION & DISCUSSION QUESTIONS

Before the Video

What Do You Think?

These are personal questions. The answers should be based on your own knowledge and experience.

Scripture Reading

- What metaphor is used to describe those who conquer? What reward is promised to them?

  The Christians in Sardis are told that those among them who conquer will be clothed in white garments. Maintaining these garments in a white and unsoiled state is a sign that the wearers are pure and worthy. Those who persevere are those who have their names written indelibly in the book of life, and Christ will speak their names in the presence of the Father and the angels.

During the Video

The Letter to Pergamum

- What are the references to "Satan's throne" and the place "where Satan dwells" in Revelation 2:13 most likely describing?

  This is likely a dual reference to the enthroned political power of Rome and the influence of pagan religion, represented by the common portrayal of Zeus seated on a throne. This double reference highlights the heightened pressure that the community of believers felt to succumb to the cultural and religious forms of idolatry around them.

- How should we understand the references to Balaam and Balak in Revelation 2:14?

  The letter to Pergamum refers to the Old Testament figure Balaam, who had been hired by Balak to pronounce a curse on the Israelites (Num. 22–24). Though he failed to curse Israel, he nevertheless showed Balak how to place a stumbling block of idolatry before the people of Israel. The reference to Balak and Balaam reveals that the same phenomenon of trying to curse the people of God and lead them astray into false worship was happening again. Jesus uses this imagery to alert the Christians of Pergamum, and indeed all Christians, to this danger.

The Letter to Thyatira

- What is the significance of the reference to Jezebel in Revelation 2:20–23?

  By referring to Jezebel in the letter to Thyatira, Jesus is comparing the impact of false teachers in Thyatira to the destructive work of Jezebel described in 1 Kings. The teachers in Thyatira who were enticing believers to follow them by offering "deep things" were, in fact, introducing error to the church just as Jezebel had introduced Baal worship to Israel centuries before.

- Why is Jesus described as having feet "like burnished bronze" in Revelation 2:18?

  The description of Jesus' feet being like burnished bronze expresses the truth that Jesus is a firm and reliable foundation. Those who rest in Him cannot be shaken. Just as Jesus does not move from the truth, He calls those who hope in Him to stand firm and not be swayed from the truth either.

The Letter to Sardis

- What is the significance of the white garments in Revelation 3:4–5?

  Jesus describes the faithful saints in Sardis as those who have not soiled their garments. Jesus, who is Himself dressed in white, praises those who walk with Him in white. They are pure and worthy because He has purified them and made them worthy. This imagery in Revelation reflects the gospel reality that those who have repented and believed in Christ are now clothed in His righteousness.

- What does the letter to Sardis say about the book of life?

  In the letter to Sardis, Jesus promises that those who overcome shall never have their names blotted out of the book of life and that He shall confess their names before the Father and the angels. This promise alludes to David's imprecatory prayer in Psalm 69:28 and anticipates the appearance of the book of life at the final judgment in Revelation 20:12–15.

After the Video

- What can we learn from the fact that the three central letters in Revelation are written to churches that are partly commended and partly rebuked? How does this inform our perspective on the body of Christ?

  Dr. Godfrey points out that the three central letters in this chiastic arrangement are addressed to churches that are faithful in some areas and in need of correction in others. This reminds us that even the faithful experience temptation and spiritual struggles. These letters give us a realistic perspective on the body of Christ, which provides us with a context to celebrate our own successes for Christ while we also pursue greater faithfulness.

- In what way is the white stone mentioned in the letter to the church at Pergamum a symbol of life in Christ?

New Testament scholar G.K. Beale suggests that the white stone is probably a reference to the jury practice of deciding whether someone was innocent or guilty. In this instance, a white stone was a symbol of the innocence of the accused. In this passage, the symbolism of the white stone affirms the righteous status in God's eyes of those who trust in Christ.

- What do the references to Balaam and the morning star in Revelation 2 reveal about God's sovereignty and sense of humor?

  In the letter to Thyatira, Jesus promises to give the morning star to those who are faithful. Interestingly, this imagery ties in to the account of Balaam alluded to in the previous letter. Though hired to curse Israel, Balaam was compelled to pronounce a blessing. In Numbers 24:17, this blessing included the messianic prophecy that "a star shall come out of Jacob, and a scepter shall rise out of Israel." This ironic twist reveals God's sovereignty. Jesus condemns Balaam in the third letter and then quotes him in the fourth, as if to say: "Balaam didn't get everything wrong. I am the Morning Star, and therefore you too will be morning stars."

REVIEW QUIZ

Lesson 5

1. **B.**
   Antipas, a member of the church in Pergamum, is mentioned by name as a faithful witness who was killed for his faith. Although unjustly put to death, he will be forever remembered by Christians because his name is mentioned in this letter.

2. **A.**
   The ancient city of Pergamum was a local Roman capital and the site of a temple to Zeus. Because of these features, it was also a place where persecution of Christians could be carried out swiftly and lethally, as indicated by the reference to the martyr Antipas. Unlike some of the cities mentioned in the seven letters, Pergamum was not located on the coast. It was situated approximately seventeen miles inland.

3. **B.**
   Dr. Godfrey summarizes the letter to Pergamum as a letter about judgment. It describes the judgment imposed on the church by Roman and pagan powers as well as the vindication that the faithful will receive in the divine courts, as evidenced by the white stone of innocence given to those who overcome.

4. **C.**
   Dr. Godfrey summarizes the letter to Thyatira as a letter about searching. Jesus identifies Himself as the Son of God who has eyes like a flame of fire. He uses them to search out who the believers in Thyatira are and to evaluate their faith and living. The searching eyes of Jesus find much to commend in these faithful believers in spite of their struggles.

5. **D.**
   The letter to Thyatira mentions the Old Testament figure Jezebel by name. She appears in this passage as a symbolic reference to someone in that church who is attempting to lead the church into idolatry.

6. **A.**
   Dr. Godfrey summarizes the letter to Sardis as a letter about holiness. Jesus issues an appeal to the believers to purify their works by repenting. Using the rich imagery of the book of life and white garments of righteousness, Christ calls the believers in Sardis to live holy lives dedicated to Him.

6

Letters to Philadelphia & Laodicea

INTRODUCTION

Jesus concludes His seven letters to the churches with a letter of encouragement to the believers in Philadelphia and a letter of rebuke to the church in Laodicea. In this lesson, Dr. Godfrey examines these final two letters, concluding the first of Revelation's seven cycles and revealing a wealth of warning, instruction, and encouragement for believers today.

LEARNING GOALS

When you have finished this lesson, you should be able to:

- Summarize the key messages of the letters to the churches in Philadelphia and Laodicea
- Navigate some of the interpretive issues that emerge in the last two letters to churches
- Articulate the overarching theme of the first cycle in the book of Revelation

KEY IDEAS

- Jesus empowers and equips His church to remain faithful in the midst of severe obstacles.
- Jesus corrects and reproves His church when it falls prey to pride and worldliness.
- Jesus remains steadfast and devoted to His church even when the future seems uncertain.

REFLECTION & DISCUSSION QUESTIONS

Before the Video

What Do You Think?

Take a moment to answer the following questions. They will prepare you for the lecture.

- When have you felt most powerless? When have you been most aware of God's power?

- How have you seen worldliness displayed in our culture? How have you seen worldliness in the church?

- Where in your life do you most need Christ's help to overcome a specific challenge?

Scripture Reading

"I am coming soon. Hold fast what you have, so that no one may seize your crown. The one who conquers, I will make him a pillar in the temple of my God. Never shall he go out of it, and I will write on him the name of my God, and the name of the city of my God, the new Jerusalem, which comes down from my God out of heaven, and my own new name."

—Revelation 3:11–12

- What does Jesus exhort the Philadelphian believers to do? What reward does He promise them?

During the Video

Answer the following questions while you watch the video. They will guide you through the lecture.

The Letter to Philadelphia *0:00–13:48*

- What is the significance of Jesus' statement that the Philadelphians "have but little power" in Revelation 3:8?

- How does Dr. Godfrey interpret the reference to the temple in Revelation 3:12?

The Letter to Laodicea *13:48–25:07*

- In what way had the church in Laodicea become worldly? How did their self-perception contrast with their spiritual reality?

- Is the book of Revelation evangelism-oriented? Why or why not?

After the Video

Answer the following questions after you have finished the lecture. They will help you identify and summarize the major points.

- How did Dr. Godfrey respond to the dispensationalist charge that his viewpoint is a form of "replacement theology"?

  If you are in a group, have the members read Psalm 87:4–5. How do these verses anticipate the full inclusion of gentiles as part of God's holy people?

- What example did Dr. Godfrey give to show how good Bible commentators can be so helpful to our study of Scripture?

  If you are in a group, have the members discuss tools and resources that they have found to be particularly helpful in their study of God's Word.

- What is Dr. Godfrey's guess about the identity of the Nicolaitans?

  If you are in a group, have the members discuss the following questions: What are the potential benefits of teasing out minute details from books like Revelation? What are the limitations or potential traps of dwelling on these details?

PRAYER

Commit what you have learned from God's Word in this lesson to prayer.

- Praise God for His perfect knowledge of the strengths and weaknesses of His people.
- Confess areas in your life where worldliness or pride has taken root.
- Thank God for remaining faithful to His church in spite of our frailty and limitations.
- Ask God to help you grow in faith and faithfulness as you fix your eyes on Jesus.

REVIEW QUIZ

Use these multiple-choice questions to measure what you learned from this lesson.

1. The letter to Philadelphia is best summarized as which of the following?
   a. Letter on faithfulness
   b. Letter on holiness
   c. Letter on judgment
   d. Letter on reproof
2. To whom does the phrase "those who dwell on the earth" usually refer in the book of Revelation?
   a. Inhabitants of the Roman province of Asia
   b. Everyone who dwells on earth
   c. Unbelievers
   d. Gentiles
3. All *except* which of the following were major industries in the city of Laodicea?
   a. Banking
   b. Medicine production
   c. Ship building
   d. Textile manufacturing
4. The letter to Laodicea is best summarized as which of the following?
   a. Letter on faithfulness
   b. Letter on holiness
   c. Letter on judgment
   d. Letter on reproof
5. The term *Nicolaitan* contains the first three letters of the Greek word for which of the following?
   a. "144,000"
   b. "Conquer"
   c. "Elect"
   d. "Suffer"
6. Which of the following best describes the overarching theme of Revelation's first cycle?
   a. Christ's acceptance of the gentiles as part of the church
   b. Christ's anger over the sins of flawed churches
   c. Christ's call to be faithful and to overcome suffering and adversity
   d. Christ's imminent return to earth

Answer Key—
Letters to Philadelphia & Laodicea

REFLECTION & DISCUSSION QUESTIONS

Before the Video

What Do You Think?

These are personal questions. The answers should be based on your own knowledge and experience.

Scripture Reading

- What does Jesus exhort the Philadelphian believers to do? What reward does He promise them?

  In His letter to the believers in Philadelphia, Jesus exhorts them to hold fast to their faith so that no one will snatch the victor's crown away from them. To the victors Jesus extends the beautiful promise of receiving the crown that will be ours because of the God who is ours.

During the Video

The Letter to Philadelphia

- What is the significance of Jesus' statement that the Philadelphians "have but little power" in Revelation 3:8?

  Jesus' statement about the power of the Philadelphian church could be taken to mean that this congregation was small numerically or that it was small in comparison to the great opposition it faced from the outside. In either case, the underlying message is that even though these believers seemed insignificant to the world, they were very significant to Jesus, who promised to bless them, preserve them, and grant them victory.

- How does Dr. Godfrey interpret the reference to the temple in Revelation 3:12?

  Jesus declares in Revelation 3:12 that those who overcome shall become pillars in the temple of God. Rather than interpreting this statement as a promise to turn people into stone, Dr. Godfrey indicates that a spiritual temple is in view. Rather than looking for a literal rebuilding of a physical temple, Dr. Godfrey and other Reformed scholars understand references to the temple in Revelation 3 and Ephesians 2 as describing the spiritual temple of which believers are a part.

The Letter to Laodicea

- In what way had the church in Laodicea become worldly? How did their self-perception contrast with their spiritual reality?

  Dr. Godfrey draws attention to G.K. Beale's scholarship to shows that the people of Laodicea took great pride in their material prosperity. Laodicea was home to the banking, textile, and medicinal industries. Rich in exports, the city had a materialistic focus that had infiltrated the church. Though these believers perceived themselves as wealthy, Christ reveals that they were impoverished in the spiritual realities that actually matter.

- Is the book of Revelation evangelism-oriented? Why or why not?

  Although there are distinct moments of evangelistic focus in the book of Revelation, Dr. Godfrey points out that the overall focus of the book is not evangelistic. Throughout the book, groups of people are depicted as being either clearly for or against Christ, with no instances of people changing sides. Instead, the primary focus of Revelation is to offer encouragement to a small group of faithful believers so that they will persist in faithfulness until Christ's return.

After the Video

- How did Dr. Godfrey respond to the dispensationalist charge that his viewpoint is a form of "replacement theology"?

  The description of covenant theology as "replacement theology" does not come from Reformed teachers. Instead, covenant theology is better described as a "fulfillment theology," in which the promises made to Old Testament Israel are understood to be fulfilled in the person and work of Jesus Christ. As a result, the gentiles now share in the blessings that God has given to the Jews with the coming of Christ. The Jews have not been displaced or replaced but are instead now joined with the gentiles to enjoy the covenant blessings that God had always intended for Jews and gentiles alike.

- What example did Dr. Godfrey give to show how good Bible commentators can be so helpful to our study of Scripture?

  While presenting the letter to the church in Laodicea, Dr. Godfrey referred to G.K. Beale's commentary on Revelation, which examined the culture and industry in Laodicea to better understand Jesus' critique of this church's worldliness. Dr. Godfrey pointed out that great Bible commentators like Beale can pick out details from the historical record that deepen our understanding of the biblical text and thereby enhance our love for God's Word.

- What is Dr. Godfrey's guess about the identity of the Nicolaitans?

  Dr. Godfrey noted that the Nicolaitans are mentioned in the first and third letters to the churches. Based on the governing structure of sevens in the book of Revelation, these letters would correspond with cycles two and four of the book, which both feature the theme of 144,000 to refer to the completeness of God's elect who are being gathered and saved. The idea communicated here is that not one of God's elect will be lost. Dr. Godfrey also noted that the name of the Nicolaitans contains the root of the Greek word for "conquer," which could indicate that the Nicolaitans were teaching that one must conquer, or remain faithful to Jesus, in order not to be lost. The juxtaposition of the Nicolaitans with the 144,000 could be a hint that the Nicolaitans taught that the number of elect was not fixed and that Christians could lose their salvation. If this is true, Nicolaitan teaching might have been an early form of Arminianism. Dr. Godfrey acknowledges that this theory is speculative at best, but it nevertheless reminds us that we are never done mining the riches of God's Word.

REVIEW QUIZ

Lesson 6

1. **A.**
   Dr. Godfrey summarizes the letter to Philadelphia as a letter on faithfulness. In this letter, Christ recognizes that the Philadelphian believers have been faithful to Him, and He calls them to continued faithfulness in the future.
2. **C.**
   Throughout the book of Revelation, the phrase "those who dwell on the earth" is used repeatedly to describe not simply the inhabitants of the earth but specifically the unbelieving inhabitants of the earth. It is a shorthand way of referring to all who are earthly minded—that is, those who do not believe in Jesus.
3. **C.**
   Banking, medicine production, and textile manufacturing were the three chief industries that contributed to the wealth of Laodicea. Due to its location far from the coast, shipbuilding was not a major industry in the city.
4. **D.**
   Dr. Godfrey summarizes the letter to Laodicea as a letter of reproof. Like the letter to Ephesus, this letter is primarily a letter of warning and correction to a church that is in grave spiritual danger.
5. **B.**
   The term Nicolaitan *contains the first three letters of the Greek word for "conquer." This forms part of the basis for Dr. Godfrey's theory that the Nicolaitan teaching may have been rooted in their vision of what it means to conquer or persevere in the faith.*
6. **C.**
   Although many important scriptural themes emerge in this first cycle of Revelation, Dr. Godfrey closes this lesson by pointing out that the dominant theme of this first cycle is Christ's call for His followers to be faithful, to persevere, to overcome, and to stand with Jesus through all circumstances.

7

The Heavenly Throne Room

INTRODUCTION

The second cycle of Revelation begins with a dazzling description of God in His glory, seated in radiant splendor on His heavenly throne. The host of heaven and the redeemed human race are fixated on Him, their every thought focused on showering Him with the praise He deserves. Amid the struggles of day-to-day life, John reminds believers that even now our God reigns. As we fix our eyes and hearts on this reality, Scripture calls us to join our hearts and voices with the heavenly chorus as it declares that God alone is holy and worthy of praise.

LEARNING GOALS

When you have finished this lesson, you should be able to:

- Describe the significance of the features and worshipers in God's heavenly throne room
- Situate the heavenly throne room scene within the larger context of Revelation

KEY IDEAS

- The triune God is holy and majestic far beyond the human capacity to describe or comprehend.
- God is seated on His throne, receiving the continuous worship of the heavenly host and the redeemed human race.
- God is to be praised for His role as Creator and Redeemer.

REFLECTION & DISCUSSION QUESTIONS

Before the Video

What Do You Think?

Take a moment to answer the following questions. They will prepare you for the lecture.

- How do you define worship? What does God desire in our worship?

- When have you most powerfully experienced the presence of God in worship?

Scripture Reading

And the four living creatures, each of them with six wings, are full of eyes all around and within, and day and night they never cease to say, "Holy, holy, holy, is the Lord God Almighty, who was and is and is to come!" And whenever the living creatures give glory and honor and thanks to him who is seated on the throne, who lives forever and ever, the twenty-four elders fall down before him who is seated on the throne and worship him who lives forever and ever. They cast their crowns before the throne, saying, "Worthy are you, our Lord and God, to receive glory and honor and power, for you created all things, and by your will they existed and were created."

—Revelation 4:8–11

- How do the living creatures and the elders worship God in these verses? What divine attributes and actions are mentioned in their praise?

During the Video

Answer the following questions while you watch the video. They will guide you through the lecture.

The Heavenly Scene *0:00–10:57*

- How do many interpreters of Revelation understand the break between Revelation 3 and Revelation 4? How does Dr. Godfrey understand this break?

- What phrase connects the temple narrative in Revelation 1 with the temple narrative in Revelation 4?

The Heavenly Worshipers *10:57–24:35*

- Who do the twenty-four elders most likely represent? Why is this important?

- What do the four living creatures most likely represent?

- How does Dr. Godfrey interpret the difference in the number of angels' wings between Ezekiel and Revelation?

After the Video

Answer the following questions after you have finished the lecture. They will help you identify and summarize the major points.

- How does John use color to communicate God's majesty in this lesson's passage?

  If you are in a group, have the members identify metaphors or word pictures they have found helpful in understanding and communicating God's holiness and glory.

- Revelation 4 contains vivid and otherworldly descriptions of heavenly beings. According to Dr. Godfrey, is it more helpful to interpret these descriptions of angelic creatures as describing their physical characteristics or their spiritual reality? What do you think?

  If you are in a group, have the members discuss what points they think are being communicated by the references to the four creatures' six wings and eyes covering their entire bodies.

- What are the themes of the two songs in Revelation 4–5? How can focusing on these themes enrich our worship?

  If you are in a group, have the members discuss particular actions and attributes of God that have been influential in how they worship Him.

PRAYER

Commit what you have learned from God's Word in this lesson to prayer.

- Praise God for His glory and majesty that surpass our ability to describe.
- Confess ways that you fall short of giving God the worship He deserves.

- Thank God for creating you and redeeming you to become part of His holy people.
- Ask God to help you cultivate a lifestyle of worshipful focus on Him.

REVIEW QUIZ

Use these multiple-choice questions to measure what you learned from this lesson.

1. Which of the following best describes the transition from Revelation 3 to Revelation 4?
   a. Continuation of the same narrative
   b. Pause between literary cycles
   c. Radical break between introduction and actual prophecy
   d. Temporal shift toward future events

2. Which of the following best describes the view of heaven presented in Revelation 1 and 4?
   a. Heaven is far away.
   b. Heaven is inaccessible.
   c. Heaven is in the future.
   d. Heaven is right now in our midst.

3. What do the crowns of the elders in the throne room symbolize?
   a. Conquering
   b. Justification
   c. Purity
   d. Royalty

4. What do the seven torches of fire in Revelation 4:5 represent?
   a. The fire of God's judgment
   b. The Holy Spirit
   c. The seven literary cycles of Revelation
   d. The seven churches

5. For which of the following was Thomas Aquinas given his nickname?
   a. His futurist interpretation of Revelation 4–5
   b. His groundbreaking commentary on Revelation
   c. His winsome personality
   d. His extensive writings about angels

6. What does the Greek word *pantokrator* mean?
   a. "Holy One"
   b. "Redeemer of all"
   c. "Ruler and Judge of all things"
   d. "The One worthy of praise"

Answer Key—The Heavenly Throne Room

REFLECTION & DISCUSSION QUESTIONS

Before the Video

What Do You Think?

These are personal questions. The answers should be based on your own knowledge and experience.

Scripture Reading

- How do the living creatures and the elders worship God in these verses? What divine attributes and actions are mentioned in their praise?

  Revelation 4 presents a stunning description of worship in the heavenly throne room. In this description, the four heavenly creatures are constantly proclaiming God's praise. In response, the twenty-four elders fall down and cast their crowns before God's throne. The songs of the creatures and elders celebrate God's eternality and worthiness to receive worship based on the fact that He is Creator of all things.

During the Video

The Heavenly Scene

- How do many interpreters of Revelation understand the break between Revelation 3 and Revelation 4? How does Dr. Godfrey understand this break?

  Many commentators—particularly those belonging to the futurist school of interpretation—view the break between Revelation 3 and 4 as a radical break that separates the first-century part of Revelation from the future, end-time portion. However, Dr. Godfrey and most Reformed commentators view it as a minor break between literary cycles. The parallel introductions to the first cycle in Revelation 1 and the second cycle in Revelation 4 indicate the continuity between these cycles, which were both intended to benefit first-century Christians as well as believers of all other generations.

- What phrase connects the temple narrative in Revelation 1 with the temple narrative in Revelation 4?

  John uses the statement "I was in the Spirit" in Revelation 1:10 and 4:2 to introduce both heavenly visions. This common verbiage establishes a thematic link between both passages.

The Heavenly Worshipers

- Who do the twenty-four elders most likely represent? Why is this important?

  The twenty-four elders in Revelation 4:4–11 represent the pairing of the twelve tribes of Israel with the twelve Apostles. This group of elders therefore represents not just twenty-four distinct individuals but rather the full array of Old Testament saints and New Testament saints joined together in one worshiping body. This is important because it demonstrates the unity of God's people throughout all of redemptive history and depicts a glorious scene in which all of redeemed humanity is joined together in worship before God's throne.

- What do the four living creatures most likely represent?

  The four living creatures described in Revelation 4:6–8 draw from the imagery of four living creatures in Ezekiel 1:5–14. Dr. Godfrey noted that these creatures most likely represent all the ranks and orders of the angelic host, just as the twenty-four elders represent all of redeemed humanity.

- How does Dr. Godfrey interpret the difference in the number of angels' wings between Ezekiel and Revelation?

  Ezekiel 1:6 records that the four living creatures each have four wings, but Revelation 4:8 reports that they each have six wings. Those who interpret these passages with wooden literalism are forced to conclude that the two accounts are describing different creatures, that the creatures acquired additional wings over time, or that one of these accounts is wrong. Instead of taking this approach, Dr. Godfrey interprets John's account as saying that the reality of these creatures is even more glorious than what Ezekiel saw.

After the Video

- How does John use color to communicate God's majesty in this lesson's passage?

  Instead of describing the heavenly throne room in terms of concrete objects and detailed physical features, John describes it in terms of radiant colors. Jasper and carnelian describe God's appearance. The area surrounding the throne is like a rainbow and an emerald, with the light of torches and a crystalline sea. The throne itself sends out bright flashes of lightning. The white color of the elders' garments symbolizes purity. The total picture that is communicated is mysterious, vivid, and overwhelmingly powerful.

- Revelation 4 contains vivid and otherworldly descriptions of heavenly beings. According to Dr. Godfrey, is it more helpful to interpret these descriptions of angelic creatures as describing their physical characteristics or their spiritual reality? What do you think?

  Dr. Godfrey suggests that the language used to describe the heavenly beings is meant to be interpreted symbolically. Rather than concluding that the four living creatures are physically covered with eyes, readers should understand the point as the creatures' comprehensive knowledge of what is taking place. Rather than concluding that the four living creatures grew additional wings between the time of Ezekiel and the time of John, readers should understand the wings as a description of their ability to move and as an indication that the glory of these beings is even greater than Ezekiel described.

- What are the themes of the two songs in Revelation 4–5? How can focusing on these themes enrich our worship?

  The first song, found in Revelation 4:8 and 4:11, is a song of creation, acknowledging that all created beings receive their life and their being from God alone. The second song, found in Revelation 5:9–13, is a song of redemption. Both of these themes should inform the worship of God's people today. God's work in creation forms the foundation of our lives and makes Him worthy of our praise. God's work in redemption also makes Him worthy to receive our praise, and it enables us to sing a new song as redeemed creatures.

REVIEW QUIZ

Lesson 7

1. **B.**
   Although many commentators see the transition between these chapters as a radical break, Dr. Godfrey points out that it is simply a transition between the end of one literary cycle and the beginning of another.

2. **D.**
   The picture of heaven presented in these chapters is of a reality that is current instead of in the future and that is in our midst instead of far away.

3. **A.**
   The crowns worn by the elders in Revelation 4 are a reference to the victor's crowns promised to those who conquer in Revelation 2:10 and 3:11. The presence of the crowns in these chapters establishes a link between these two literary cycles; the saints in the heavenly throne room are the same ones who are encouraged to persevere in the letters to the seven churches.

4. **B.**
   The seven torches represent the seven spirits of God mentioned in chapter 1. As Dr. Godfrey pointed out earlier, these spirits represent the perfection and completion of the Holy Spirit in His ministry to God's people.

5. **D.**
   Thomas Aquinas, the renowned medieval theologian, is sometimes referred to as "the Angelic Doctor." He received this nickname not because of his personality but because of his extensive writing on the topic of angels.

6. **C.**
   Revelation 4:8 describes God as "Almighty" using the Greek word pantokrator, *which means "Ruler and Judge of all things."*

8

Worthy Is the Lamb

INTRODUCTION

After describing the breathtaking glory of the worship taking place in God's throne room, John presents a grave conundrum. In God's hand rests a scroll that holds the future of the human race, yet no one is present who is able to open it. Just as John begins to despair, he finds hope in the Lamb of God, who alone is worthy to open the scroll and consummate God's design for human history. In this lesson, Dr. Godfrey will explore this dramatic heavenly scene and revel in the glorious hope that we have in the ever-worthy Lamb of God, Jesus Christ.

LEARNING GOALS

When you have finished this lesson, you should be able to:

- Explain the significance of the scroll and why only Jesus can open it
- Describe the four horsemen of the apocalypse and their role in Revelation
- Articulate the Christian hope that is made possible in Christ

KEY IDEAS

- Because Jesus is the Lamb who was slain, He is worthy to open the scroll of history.
- The four horsemen of the apocalypse reveal the tragedy of life in a fallen world.
- The hope of the Christian is a new heaven and a new earth where we shall reign with Christ in peace, righteousness, and holiness.

REFLECTION & DISCUSSION QUESTIONS

Before the Video

What Do You Think?

Take a moment to answer the following questions. They will prepare you for the lecture.

- What are some of the most significant events of human history? How has Jesus influenced human history in the past? How is Jesus involved in shaping human history today?

- Is suffering normal or abnormal to human life? Why?

Scripture Reading

Then I looked, and I heard around the throne and the living creatures and the elders the voice of many angels, numbering myriads of myriads and thousands of thousands, saying with a loud voice, "Worthy is the Lamb who was slain, to receive power and wealth and wisdom and might and honor and glory and blessing!" And I heard every creature in heaven and on earth and under the earth and in the sea, and all that is in them, saying, "To him who sits on the throne and to the Lamb be blessing and honor and glory and might forever and ever!" And the four living creatures said, "Amen!" and the elders fell down and worshiped.

—Revelation 5:11–14

- What categories of creatures participate in the worship described in these verses? What attributes are ascribed to the Lamb? What do these verses imply about the divinity of Jesus?

During the Video

Answer the following questions while you watch the video. They will guide you through the lecture.

The Lamb and the Scroll *0:00–16:08*

- What expectation is created in Revelation 5:5 by the mention of One who is worthy to open the scroll? How is this expectation turned upside down?

- According to Revelation 5:9–10, why is Jesus qualified to open the scroll?

The Four Horsemen of the Apocalypse *16:08–24:23*

- What comes out of the scroll of history? How is this accurate to human experience?

- What point does Dr. Godfrey make about the sequential presentation of the horses in this passage?

After the Video

Answer the following questions after you have finished the lecture. They will help you identify and summarize the major points.

- What symbolism does John use in Revelation 5:8 to describe the prayers of God's people? What does this symbolism say about how God views prayer?

  If you are in a group, have the members describe the aromas that are most pleasing to them. How might this reminder affect your prayer life?

- What is the true hope of the Christian, as described in Revelation 5:10?

  If you are in a group, have the members interact with Dr. Godfrey's summary of the Christian hope. Is this accurate? Why or why not? How would you describe the Christian hope in your own words?

- What does Dr. Godfrey make of the juxtaposition of the glory of Revelation 5 with the misery of Revelation 6?

  If you are in a group, have the members discuss a time they have come face-to-face with the power and majesty of God and a time when they vividly encountered human misery.

PRAYER

Commit what you have learned from God's Word in this lesson to prayer.

- Praise Jesus, the Lamb of God, for being worthy to open the scroll of human history.
- Confess factors in your life that take you away from spending time in prayer.
- Thank God for being present with His people and receiving their prayers even in times of hardship and suffering.
- Ask God to empower you to live prayerfully and hopefully in a world filled with despair.

REVIEW QUIZ

Use these multiple-choice questions to measure what you learned from this lesson.

1. What does the scroll in the right hand of God represent?
   a. Angelic praise
   b. Divine attributes
   c. Human history
   d. Prayers of the saints
2. Which of the following symbolizes the prayers of the saints?
   a. Bowls of incense
   b. Golden lampstands
   c. Seals on the scroll
   d. Seven horns and seven eyes
3. According to Revelation 5:9, which of the following qualifies Jesus to open the scroll?
   a. Being fully human and fully divine
   b. Dying to ransom people for God
   c. Fulfilling messianic prophecies
   d. Rising from the dead
4. Which name or title is used most frequently to refer to Jesus throughout Revelation?
   a. "Christ"
   b. "Jesus"
   c. "Lamb"
   d. "Son of Man"
5. The Apostle Paul refers to Jesus as the "Lamb" more than any other biblical author.
   a. True
   b. False
6. Which of the following best describes the function of the four horsemen of the apocalypse?
   a. Beginning of final judgment
   b. Heralds of divine blessing
   c. Metaphor for the seven-year great tribulation
   d. Representation of ordinary human life

Answer Key—Worthy Is the Lamb

REFLECTION & DISCUSSION QUESTIONS

Before the Video

What Do You Think?

These are personal questions. The answers should be based on your own knowledge and experience.

Scripture Reading

- What categories of creatures participate in the worship described in these verses? What attributes are ascribed to the Lamb? What do these verses imply about the divinity of Jesus?

  These verses describe acts of worship carried out by a vast angelic host, followed by all heavenly and earthly creatures, followed by the four living creatures that represent celestial beings, and concluding with the twenty-four elders that represent the totality of the redeemed people of God. The chorus of all creatures ascribes blessing, honor, glory, and might to Jesus. The angelic voices mentioned all of those attributes along with power, wealth, and wisdom. The mention of divine attributes that both the One seated on the throne (the Father) and the Lamb (the Son) possess, coupled with the fact that both receive the worship of the assembly, is a strong statement of Christ's divinity.

During the Video

The Lamb and the Scroll

- What expectation is created in Revelation 5:5 by the mention of One who is worthy to open the scroll? How is this expectation turned upside down?

  Revelation 5:5 introduces the One who is worthy to open the scroll in terms of some of the greatest messianic promises of the Old Testament. The references to the Lion of the tribe of Judah, the Root of David, and One who has conquered create the expectation of strength and power. Instead of following through on these expectations by revealing a mighty warrior, John's vision shows a symbol of defeat, a Lamb that looks as it if has been slain.

- According to Revelation 5:9–10, why is Jesus qualified to open the scroll?

  Jesus' qualification to open the scroll of human history is the fact that He was slain, that with His blood He has ransomed a people for God from every nation, that He is making them into a kingdom of priests, and that they shall reign on the earth.

The Four Horsemen of the Apocalypse

- What comes out of the scroll of history? How is this accurate to human experience?

  Dr. Godfrey observed that when the scroll—representing human history—is opened, misery emerges. Instead of bringing the peace and prosperity that is hoped for, human history is characterized by war, famine, and death. Though disheartening, this depiction of human history in Revelation is consistent with human experience because it describes what life is really like in a fallen world.

- What point does Dr. Godfrey make about the sequential presentation of the horses in this passage?

  The presentation of the four horsemen of the apocalypse in Revelation 6:1–8 illustrates Revelation's literary characteristic of presenting things that occur at the same time in a staggered sequence. Some may view the sequential presentation of the horsemen as if they appear one after another in human history, yet the reality is that they are described one at a time but tend to surface as one complete package in the present evil age.

After the Video

- What symbolism does John use in Revelation 5:8 to describe the prayers of God's people? What does this symbolism say about how God views prayer?

  Revelation 5:8 identifies the golden bowls of incense in the throne room as the prayers of the saints. Just as the smoke from the incense rises up with a sweet smell, so the prayers of God's people bring a pleasing aroma to God as they rise before His throne. He recognizes, honors, and delights in the prayers of His children.

- What is the true hope of the Christian, as described in Revelation 5:10?

  Revelation 5:10 celebrates Christ's act of rescuing a people to become a kingdom of priests who shall reign on the earth. Reflecting on this verse, Dr. Godfrey notes that the true hope of the Christian is not simply heaven. Rather, the hope of the Christian is a new heaven and a new earth where we shall dwell in righteousness. The hope of the Christian is not just the redemption of the soul but rather the redemption of the body and the renewal of life on earth as it was intended by God to be lived.

- What does Dr. Godfrey make of the juxtaposition of the glory of Revelation 5 with the misery of Revelation 6?

  In keeping with the principle that Revelation describes present realities, Dr. Godfrey points out that Revelation 5 and 6 first portray God's glory in all its fullness and then dramatically shift focus to describe intense human suffering. In spite of this abrupt shift, these realities are not contradictory. The present reality is one in which God's glory is beautifully displayed in heaven, and human misery is radically rampant on earth. Our future hope is for a day when heaven and earth are brought together, and both are filled with the glory of God.

REVIEW QUIZ

Lesson 8

1. **C.**
   The scroll in God's right hand represents human history. John is moved to tears when no one is present to open it because this would symbolize the tragedy of human history without meaning or resolution.

2. **A.**
   Revelation 5:8 explicitly identifies the golden bowls of incense with the prayers of God's people. This verse beautifully portrays the sweet aroma that God enjoys when the prayers of His children rise before Him.

3. **B.**
   Though each of these options states something true about the person and work of Christ, the song of redemption in Revelation 5:9 celebrates the fact that Jesus is worthy to open the scroll because He was slain and ransomed people for God with His blood.

4. **C.**
   The book of Revelation uses the word "Lamb" twenty-eight times to refer to Jesus as the Lamb of God. This is a wonderful reminder to us of Jesus' conquering through His sacrificial death on behalf of His people.

5. **B.**
   Of all the New Testament writers, John, who used this title twenty-eight times in the book of Revelation alone, uses the designation "Lamb" to refer to Jesus more than any other.

6. **D.**
   Although the four horsemen of the apocalypse are often viewed as harbingers of final judgment, Dr. Godfrey points out that they actually serve as a representation of the ordinary way that life works out in this world. Famine, war, suffering, and death are sadly the norm in a fallen world.

9

Salvation Belongs to the Lord

INTRODUCTION

As we continue to examine the seven seals that John describes in the second cycle of the book of Revelation, God's Word invites us to wrestle with challenging questions. In all ages, God's people cry out, "How long, O Lord?" If God is in control, why is evil allowed to endure? Why is Jesus taking so long to return? In this lesson, Dr. Godfrey will navigate these questions and others, concluding that God is indeed in control, that salvation belongs to Him, and that even now He is at work in rescuing His people from darkness and despair.

LEARNING GOALS

When you have finished this lesson, you should be able to:

- Summarize the meaning of the fifth and sixth seals in the second cycle of Revelation
- Express a longing for Christ's return, an understanding of why it has not happened yet, and a certainty that Christ's victory will one day be complete

KEY IDEAS

- Christians in every century await Christ's return with eagerness, to see wickedness punished and all that is wrong set right.
- As we await Christ's return, God is rescuing His elect from the power of sin and death.
- At Christ's return, justice will be carried out against the wicked, and God's people will joyously celebrate the victory of the Lamb.

REFLECTION & DISCUSSION QUESTIONS

Before the Video

What Do You Think?

Take a moment to answer the following questions. They will prepare you for the lecture.

- What will heaven be like? What might be the primary emotions believers experience in heaven as they wait to be bodily raised from the dead?

- Would you prefer for Jesus to return in the near future or in the distant future? Why?

Scripture Reading

Oh Lord, God of vengeance, O God of vengeance, shine forth! Rise up, O judge of the earth; repay to the proud what they deserve! O Lord, how long shall the wicked, how long shall the wicked exult? They pour out their arrogant words; all the evildoers boast. They crush your people, O Lord, and afflict your heritage. They kill the widow and the sojourner and murder the fatherless; and they say, "The Lord does not see, the God of Jacob does not perceive."

—Psalm 94:1–7

- What longing is expressed in these verses? What is the attitude of the wicked toward God and toward His people?

During the Video

Answer the following questions while you watch the video. They will guide you through the lecture.

The Fifth Seal *0:00–9:07*

- According to the description of the fifth seal, what is the reason that history goes on? What is the problem with history going on?

- What is the central message of Revelation's second cycle?

The Sixth Seal *9:07–25:13*

- How does the first scene of the sixth seal answer the plea of the martyrs in the fifth seal?

- According to the second scene of the sixth seal, why has the final judgment not yet come?

- How does the third scene of the sixth seal lead back into the heavenly throne room?

After the Video

Answer the following questions after you have finished the lecture. They will help you identify and summarize the major points.

- How does the picture of the saints in heaven presented in Revelation 6:9–11 differ from the way that most people envision heaven?

  If you are in a group, have the members describe the way they usually hear heaven depicted. How does this passage reinforce your previous beliefs about heaven? How does it challenge them?

- Read Psalm 94:23 and Matthew 28:18–20. What can Christians learn from the tension in the Bible between desiring judgment on the wicked and desiring repentance and forgiveness for them?

  If you are in a group, have the members describe ways that they personally experience this tension between wanting the wicked to be punished and wanting them to repent and believe.

- How does the sixth seal of Revelation connect with the doctrine of baptism?

  If you are in a group, have the members discuss the Christian life. If you have been purchased by the blood of Christ, what should your life look like?

PRAYER

Commit what you have learned from God's Word in this lesson to prayer.

- Praise God for His sovereign work in gathering His elect throughout human history.

- Confess personal discouragement or doubts about God's justice being carried out.
- Thank God for His unwavering commitment to both justice and mercy.
- Ask God to continue to change the hearts of sinners as He gathers His elect.

REVIEW QUIZ

Use these multiple-choice questions to measure what you learned from this lesson.

1. Which of the following best describes the attitude of the saints in heaven in Revelation 6:9–11?
   a. Angry
   b. Content
   c. Joyful
   d. Restless

2. To desire God's judgment on the wicked is an unbiblical attitude because Jesus calls believers to love their enemies.
   a. True
   b. False

3. The first scene of the sixth seal presents a picture of which of the following?
   a. Celebration
   b. Evangelism
   c. Judgment
   d. Mercy

4. The second scene of the sixth seal presents a picture of which of the following?
   a. Evangelism
   b. Judgment
   c. Mercy
   d. Perseverance

5. Which of the following conclusions does Dr. Godfrey *not* draw from the list of 144,000 sealed from twelve tribes?
   a. Belonging to a family or church does not guarantee a person's salvation.
   b. Devout Jews will be saved regardless of their messianic beliefs.
   c. Israel is not abandoned; Jews will continue to be brought to faith.
   d. Those who accept Christ as the Messiah are the true Jews.

6. The third scene of the sixth seal presents a picture of which of the following?
   a. Celebration
   b. Faith
   c. Judgment
   d. Mercy

Answer Key—
Salvation Belongs to the Lord

REFLECTION & DISCUSSION QUESTIONS

Before the Video

What Do You Think?

These are personal questions. The answers should be based on your own knowledge and experience.

Scripture Reading

- What longing is expressed in these verses? What is the attitude of the wicked toward God and toward His people?

  These verses express the longing of the righteous to see justice fall on evildoers whose wicked deeds appear to have gone unpunished. The psalmist is particularly burdened by the malicious behavior of the wicked toward God's people, whom they are afflicting without mercy. Undergirding this oppressive behavior is the assumption on the part of the wicked that God is not aware of their evil deeds and will not do anything to bring them to justice.

During the Video

The Fifth Seal

- According to the description of the fifth seal, what is the reason that history goes on? What is the problem with history going on?

  Revelation 6:11 urges Christian martyrs who are crying out for justice to wait a little longer until the full number of their fellow servants is complete. This section indicates that there is a reason why Jesus has not returned yet. Human history is allowed to continue so that the full number of God's elect can be gathered from all nations, tribes, tongues, and times. While the gathering of the elect is a beautiful reality, the perpetuation of human history brings with it the continued problem of sin, suffering, misery, and martyrdom.

- What is the central message of Revelation's second cycle?

  Dr. Godfrey pointed out that the central message of the second cycle is to explain why the righteous suffer and what the character of their suffering is all about. This cycle encourages God's people to endure that suffering because it has a great purpose to honor God and allow time for the gathering of God's elect.

The Sixth Seal

- How does the first scene of the sixth seal answer the plea of the martyrs in the fifth seal?

  The narrative of the fifth seal describes the martyrs' asking how long they must wait before justice is carried out against the wicked who oppressed and killed them. In response to the martyrs' outcry, the sixth seal begins with a vivid description of God's judgment being poured out on the rich and powerful. Thus, the sixth seal assures the martyrs that divine justice will not be delayed forever.

- According to the second scene of the sixth seal, why has the final judgment not yet come?

  The second scene of the sixth seal describes angels who are restraining the winds of judgment until the 144,000 servants of God have received His seal on their foreheads. The message conveyed in this passage is that God's judgment is being suspended until all of God's elect have been sealed and gathered.

- How does the third scene of the sixth seal lead back into the heavenly throne room?

  Revelation 7:9, which opens the third scene of the sixth seal, describes a great multitude that is standing before the throne in the presence of the angels, the four living creatures, and the elders mentioned in Revelation 4 and 5. This heavenly multitude, made up of the elect whom God is gathering in the second scene, joins in the throne room setting that formed the introduction to the second cycle of Revelation. In this way, the second cycle begins in the throne room and returns there to expand the vision of glorious worship that takes place in God's presence.

After the Video

- How does the picture of the saints in heaven presented in Revelation 6:9–11 differ from the way that most people envision heaven?

  Most Christians think of heaven as a place where believers are relieved of all of life's burdens to enjoy perfect contentment, joy, and bliss. While this picture accurately conveys the biblical belief that Christians will experience joy and rest in the Lord's presence after death, Revelation 6:9–11 indicates that believers in heaven still experience a lingering sense of restlessness and incompleteness as they await the fulfillment of divine justice and the perfection of a new heaven and a new earth.

- Read Psalm 94:23 and Matthew 28:18–20. What can Christians learn from the tension in the Bible between desiring judgment on the wicked and desiring repentance and forgiveness for them?

  Psalm 94:23 answers the psalmist's cry for justice with the assurance that the wicked will be justly punished for their sins. On the other hand, Jesus calls us to disciple the nations in the Great Commission in Matthew 28. These verses, and others, illustrate the biblical dilemma between wanting the wicked to be punished and wanting them to repent. The overall message of Scripture is that Christians must keep both of these perspectives in balance. We must genuinely love our enemies and desire them to repent, but we also look with longing for the day when justice will be fulfilled.

- How does the sixth seal of Revelation connect with the doctrine of baptism?

  The reference to God's servants receiving His seal on their foreheads evokes the imagery of baptism, which is the seal of God's new covenant administered to the visible church. This covenant seal offers great encouragement to God's people of His enduring promise and favor upon them.

REVIEW QUIZ

Lesson 9

1. **D.**
   Although one might expect the experience of saints in heaven to be characterized by unbridled joy, Revelation 6:9–11 describes the martyred saints as restless, crying out for God to fulfill His promises in human history.

2. **B.**
   The longing for judgment is legitimate and scriptural since judgment is righteousness. Jesus' command to love one's enemy is motivated by a desire to see the wicked repent and receive new life in Christ. When evildoers persist in doing evil, it is appropriate for the righteous to desire to see justice done.

3. **C.**
   In response to the outcry of the martyrs for justice, the first scene of the sixth seal reveals the judgment that will one day fall on the earth. On that day, justice will finally be carried out against those who have oppressed and killed the saints.

4. **A.**
   The second scene of the sixth seal offers a picture of evangelism taking place. God's judgment on the earth is being delayed to allow time for the full number of God's elect to be gathered from every nation.

5. **B.**
   Dr. Godfrey observes that the teaching about the 144,000 from twelve tribes who are sealed indicates (1) that Jews are not simply abandoned by God but continue to be led to faith in Christ, (2) that all who confess Christ as Lord and Savior are true Jews, and (3) that merely belonging to a family or church does not guarantee salvation. Salvation comes by faith alone through grace alone in Christ alone. Those who faithfully follow Jewish religious teachings, no matter how devout, will perish in their sins apart from Christ.

6. **A.**
   The third and final scene of the sixth seal portrays a great day of celebration when the multitude of the redeemed joins in the worship around God's throne and cries out with a loud voice that salvation belongs to the Lord.

10

From Seals to Trumpets

INTRODUCTION

After John revels in the sight of the great multitude from every nation in praise of God in the heavenly throne room, the focus once more turns back to tribulation and suffering. In contrast with the rejoicing of God's people who have emerged victorious from their earthly troubles, the cycle that follows speaks of the even greater suffering experienced by the unbelieving earth. As we move from the seals of the second cycle to the trumpets of the third cycle, Dr. Godfrey will point out key insights to help us better have a heavenly view of the suffering we see around us.

LEARNING GOALS

When you have finished this lesson, you should be able to:

- Summarize the meaning of the seventh seal in the second cycle of Revelation
- Summarize the meaning of the first four trumpets in the third cycle of Revelation
- Describe the similarities and differences between Revelation's second and third cycles

KEY IDEAS

- Even in the midst of suffering, Christians can trust that God's purposes will prevail and that our present suffering will seem brief in hindsight.
- When Christians experience or observe suffering, the proper response is repentance and a renewed clinging to Christ.

REFLECTION & DISCUSSION QUESTIONS

Before the Video

What Do You Think?

Take a moment to answer the following questions. They will prepare you for the lecture.

- In what kinds of situations does time seem to pass quickly? In what kinds of situations does time seem to pass slowly?

- What comes to mind when you think of repentance? Describe a time when you repented of something.

Scripture Reading

Then one of the elders addressed me, saying, "Who are these, clothed in white robes, and from where have they come?" I said to him, "Sir, you know." And he said to me, "These are the ones coming out of the great tribulation. They have washed their robes and made them white in the blood of the Lamb. Therefore they are before the throne of God, and serve him day and night in his temple; and he who sits on the throne will shelter them with his presence. They shall hunger no more, neither thirst anymore; the sun shall not strike them, nor any scorching heat. For the Lamb in the midst of the throne will be their shepherd, and he will guide them to springs of living water, and God will wipe away every tear from their eyes."

—Revelation 7:13–17

- What imagery from other parts of Revelation and other Scripture passages appears in these verses? What hope does this passage offer to God's people?

During the Video

Answer the following questions while you watch the video. They will guide you through the lecture.

The Final Seals *0:00–11:00*

- What is meant by the phrase "the great tribulation" in Revelation 7:14?

- According to Dr. Godfrey, how is the seventh seal to be understood?

The First Five Trumpets *11:00–25:27*

- What specific prayers are likely in view when Revelation 8:3–4 again mentions the prayers of the saints?

- How does Dr. Godfrey interpret the differing percentages of the earth destroyed in cycles 2 and 3?

After the Video

Answer the following questions after you have finished the lecture. They will help you identify and summarize the major points.

- How does Dr. Godfrey describe the difference between the seals and the trumpets? How does this difference distinguish cycles 2 and 3 of Revelation?

  If you are in a group, have the members discuss which concept from cycle 2 (the seals) they consider to be most meaningful to believers, and which concept from cycle 3 (the trumpets) they consider to be most significant to unbelievers.

- One of the dominant themes of cycle 3 is the suffering of the wicked in history. In your opinion, how should Christians respond to the suffering of unbelievers?

  If you are in a group, have the members share an example of (1) a time when Christians responded well to the suffering of others and (2) a time when Christians responded poorly to the suffering of others.

- How does the quote that Dr. Godfrey read from a nineteenth-century commentary illustrate the outlandish interpretive approaches that people can take to Revelation?

  If you are in a group, have the members reflect on and discuss their experience of different approaches to studying the book of Revelation. What things have members read or heard that have been helpful in understanding this book? What things have members read or heard that have been unhelpful?

PRAYER

Commit what you have learned from God's Word in this lesson to prayer.

- Praise God for providing warnings in history and Scripture to lead to repentance.
- Confess areas of your life where you need to repent and refocus on God.

- Thank God for lovingly leading you to repent of sin and believe in Christ.
- Ask God to use this study of Revelation to make you more humble, pure, and holy.

REVIEW QUIZ

Use these multiple-choice questions to measure what you learned from this lesson.

1. Which of the following best describes the great tribulation of Revelation 7:14?
   a. Nero's reign
   b. Period of intense evil before Christ's return
   c. Seven years after the rapture
   d. Suffering of Christians throughout history

2. What is the content of the seventh seal?
   a. Bowls of incense
   b. Horsemen
   c. Silence
   d. Trumpets

3. What kind of message do the trumpets of Revelation 8–11 symbolize?
   a. God's guarantee to the righteous
   b. God's warning to the wicked
   c. Judgment on the righteous and wicked alike
   d. The prayers of the saints

4. The first four trumpets describe the destruction of what portion of creation?
   a. One-half
   b. One-third
   c. One-fourth
   d. One-seventh

5. According to Dr. Godfrey, what is the best response to suffering in history?
   a. Informing people why they are suffering
   b. Repenting of our sins
   c. Satisfaction in our own righteousness
   d. Urging unbelievers to repent

6. The locusts from the pit in Revelation 9:3–10 most likely represent which of the following?
   a. An army from hell
   b. Helicopters
   c. Horsemen with repeating rifles
   d. Radiation

Answer Key—From Seals to Trumpets

REFLECTION & DISCUSSION QUESTIONS

Before the Video

What Do You Think?

These are personal questions. The answers should be based on your own knowledge and experience.

Scripture Reading

- What imagery from other parts of Revelation and other Scripture passages appears in these verses? What hope does this passage offer to God's people?

  These verses are replete with biblical imagery. The reference to the white robes points back to the letter to Sardis in Revelation 3:4, the raiment of the twenty-four elders in 4:4, and the robes given to the martyrs in 6:11. The promise that God will wipe every tear from their eyes anticipates the joy of the new Jerusalem in Revelation 21:4. The promise that they shall hunger and thirst no more reflects the words of Jesus in Matthew 5:6: "Blessed are those who hunger and thirst for righteousness, for they shall be satisfied." The promise that Jesus will be their shepherd draws a connection to Psalm 23. All in all, these verses assure God's people that He will fulfill His promise to return, consummate His kingdom on earth, and dwell with His people forever.

During the Video

The Final Seals

- What is meant by the phrase "the great tribulation" in Revelation 7:14?

  The phrase "the great tribulation" in Revelation 7:14 simply refers to a period of great travail. This phrase points back to John's comment in Revelation 1:9 that he is the partner of the believers in the kingdom and in tribulation. These references to tribulation in the lives of Christians reiterate the idea that the life of faith in an unbelieving world is characterized by struggle. Tribulation, therefore, is an ever-present reality in the experience of Christians throughout history.

- According to Dr. Godfrey, how is the seventh seal to be understood?

  Although some commentators conclude that the seventh seal includes the seven trumpets, Dr. Godfrey contends that the seals and trumpets are distinct cycles. Instead, the seventh seal is simply the half hour of silence that permeated the heavenly throne room. The point of this silence is an illustration of the fact that even a short duration of time seems to take much longer when one is waiting in silence. In the same way, the period of time when God's people await Christ's return seems like forever but in hindsight will be remembered as quite brief.

The First Five Trumpets

- What specific prayers are likely in view when Revelation 8:3–4 again mentions the prayers of the saints?

  In Revelation 8, John repeats his earlier statement that the bowls of incense in the throne room are the prayers of the saints. This is true in general of the prayers of all God's people. Yet, the specific outcry of the martyrs—"How long?"—is most likely in view in this instance. This repetition reminds us that the martyrs' cry for justice has not been forgotten.

- How does Dr. Godfrey interpret the differing percentages of the earth destroyed in cycles 2 and 3?

  In the second cycle, which is directed primarily to believers, the four horsemen of the apocalypse destroy one-fourth of the earth. In the third cycle, which is directed primarily to unbelievers, the parallel trumpets of judgment describe the destruction of one-third of the earth. Dr. Godfrey understands the difference in percentages to be a response to the perception of suffering Christians that they suffer more than the wicked. The greater percentage of destruction in the passage directed to unbelievers makes the point that, despite appearances to the contrary, the wicked suffer more.

After the Video

- How does Dr. Godfrey describe the difference between the seals and the trumpets? How does this difference distinguish cycles 2 and 3 of Revelation?

  Cycles 2 and 3 of Revelation are parallel to each other in many ways. Dr. Godfrey describes their difference in terms of the difference between seals and trumpets: seals convey God's guarantee, and trumpets raise the alarm. Cycle 2, organized around the seven seals, describes God's guarantee of protection over the righteous even in the midst of their suffering in history. Cycle 3 describes similar events but from the perspective of issuing a warning to the unconverted.

- One of the dominant themes of cycle 3 is the suffering of the wicked in history. In your opinion, how should Christians respond to the suffering of unbelievers?

  The answers to these questions should take into consideration Dr. Godfrey's points about not rejoicing in the misfortunes of others, about learning from history, and about responding to tragedy through repentance.

- How does the quote that Dr. Godfrey read from a nineteenth-century commentary illustrate the outlandish interpretive approaches that people can take to Revelation?

Dr. Godfrey referred to a commentary that had claimed that the nineteenth-century invention of a repeating rifle had fulfilled the description of the locusts from the pit in Revelation 9 because a person could now ride on horseback and fire backward. This quote illustrates the danger of looking for contemporary, literal fulfillments of statements that were meant to be interpreted symbolically in a first-century context.

REVIEW QUIZ

Lesson 10

1. **D.**
   The phrase "great tribulation" in Revelation 7:14 does not refer to a specific period of evil at the end of history but rather refers to the entire experience of believers' suffering throughout history.

2. **C.**
   Although some commentators identify the seventh seal with the seven trumpets, Dr. Godfrey points out that the thirty minutes of silence in heaven is not a prelude to the content of the seventh seal but is actually the content of the seventh seal.

3. **B.**
   Although Revelation's presentation of the seven trumpets contains many parallels to the guarantee of protection offered to the righteous in the cycle of the seven seals, the trumpets primarily represent a warning to unbelievers.

4. **B.**
   The first four trumpets, described in Revelation 8:7–12, depict the destruction of one-third of various features of creation, such as trees, grass, seas, rivers, sun, moon, and stars.

5. **B.**
   Dr. Godfrey reminds us in this lecture that the Christian's primary response to suffering in the world should be personal repentance. This repentance, in turn, ought to lead to godly and compassionate behavior toward those who suffer.

6. **A.**
   Instead of trying to interpret the locusts from the pit as a clouded reference to future military technology, Dr. Godfrey argues that the locusts are best interpreted as a symbolic reference to an army from hell—that is, an army of evil powers unleashed to wreak havoc on the earth.

11

Fifth & Sixth Trumpets

INTRODUCTION

As the third literary cycle continues to describe judgment poured out on the earth, some difficult questions emerge. When the forces of evil appear to be so strong, how do we know that God is greater? In the face of intense suffering, why do more people not turn to Jesus? Why has God chosen to reveal some parts of His plan but not others? In this lesson, Dr. Godfrey will examine these questions and other complex features of these passages, finding hope in God's sovereign power and faithful care for His people.

LEARNING GOALS

When you have finished this lesson, you should be able to:

- Summarize the meaning of the fifth and sixth trumpets in the third cycle of Revelation
- Understand and describe some of the rich and complex imagery in Revelation 9–11

KEY IDEAS

- Despite appearances to the contrary, God's power and strength are far greater than that of human governments and demonic forces.
- In spite of God's mighty acts in human history, some will choose never to repent and turn to Him.
- God has chosen to reveal many parts of His redemptive plan and has also chosen not to reveal some details that we wish we knew.

REFLECTION & DISCUSSION QUESTIONS

Before the Video

What Do You Think?

Take a moment to answer the following questions. They will prepare you for the lecture.

- When it comes to the way the world is today, does it seem as if God is winning, or does it seem as if evil is winning? Explain your answer.

- When you think about the current state of the church, culture, and human life, what do you find discouraging? What encourages you?

Scripture Reading

Why should the nations say, "Where is their God?" Our God is in the heavens; he does all that he pleases. Their idols are silver and gold, the work of human hands. They have mouths, but do not speak; eyes, but do not see. They have ears, but do not hear; noses, but do not smell. They have hands, but do not feel; feet, but do not walk; and they do not make a sound in their throat. Those who make them become like them; so do all who trust in them.

—Psalm 115:2–8

- How do these verses describe the difference between the God of the Bible and the "gods" of the nations? What is the result of worshiping these false gods?

During the Video

Answer the following questions while you watch the video. They will guide you through the lecture.

The Two Armies *0:00–11:45*

- How is God's army described in Revelation 9:13–19? How does the devil's army compare to God's army?

- According to Revelation 9:20–21, how does the rest of humanity respond to the suffering and judgment the wicked experience?

Echoes of Ezekiel *11:45–25:46*

- How does the third scene of the sixth trumpet refer the reader back to the book of Ezekiel?

- Is the temple described in Revelation 11 a physical building or a spiritual reality? Explain.

After the Video

Answer the following questions after you have finished the lecture. They will help you identify and summarize the major points.

- How does Revelation 9 acknowledge the disheartening reality that, in spite of having access to God's truth, unbelievers so often persist in their unbelief?

  If you are in a group, have the members describe an experience of trying to share the gospel with someone who shows little interest in Jesus. Take a few minutes to pray for these individuals.

- What is the difference between the big scroll of Revelation 5:1 and the little scroll of Revelation 10:2? What does this difference teach us about how God reveals His plans to us?

  If you are in a group, have the members read Deuteronomy 29:29. What is central to what God has revealed to us in the context of Deuteronomy? What are some implications of this?

- How should we understand the reference to three and a half years in Revelation 11? How does this apply to the church's experience?

  If you are in a group, have the members reflect on times of waiting, difficulty, or uncertainty in their lives. In what ways was God's timing different from yours? How did you come to see part of a larger purpose in God's timing?

PRAYER

Commit what you have learned from God's Word in this lesson to prayer.

- Praise God for His sovereignty over human history and all earthly and spiritual forces.
- Confess how you struggle to trust or follow Him in times of uncertainty.

- Thank God for revealing enough of His plan to encourage and guide His people.
- Ask God to give you courage, endurance, and joy as you follow Jesus.

REVIEW QUIZ

Use these multiple-choice questions to measure what you learned from this lesson.

1. Which two rivers formed the boundaries of the ancient Near East?
   a. Jordan and Nile
   b. Nile and Euphrates
   c. Orontes and Jordan
   d. Tigris and Euphrates

2. At most, the population of the Roman Empire in the first century was approximately how large?
   a. 200,000
   b. 2,000,000
   c. 20,000,000
   d. 200,000,000

3. What imagery describes the tails of the horses ridden by God's army in Revelation 9?
   a. Chariots in battle
   b. Lion heads
   c. Scorpion tails
   d. Serpent heads

4. What was John instructed to do immediately after the seven thunders sounded?
   a. Eat a scroll
   b. Prophesy about many nations, peoples, and kings
   c. Seal up and not write down what the seven thunders said
   d. Write down what the seven thunders said

5. What is the content of the little scroll in Revelation 10:2?
   a. Details about human history that God has chosen not to reveal
   b. God's overarching plan of redemption in Christ
   c. Letters to seven churches
   d. Warning to unbelievers to repent

6. According to Dr. Godfrey, which temple is being measured in Revelation 11?
   a. Heavenly temple
   b. Herod's temple
   c. Millennial temple
   d. Solomon's temple

Answer Key—Fifth & Sixth Trumpets

REFLECTION & DISCUSSION QUESTIONS

Before the Video

What Do You Think?

These are personal questions. The answers should be based on your own knowledge and experience.

Scripture Reading

- How do these verses describe the difference between the God of the Bible and the "gods" of the nations? What is the result of worshiping these false gods?

  In these verses, the psalmist contrasts the God of Israel, who dwells in the heavens and has the power to do all that pleases Him, with the lifeless idols of the surrounding nations. These idols are made by human hands and resemble the human form without any ability to think, feel, see, speak, or move. According to this passage, the result of worshiping lifeless gods is that the worshipers become lifeless themselves.

During the Video

The Two Armies

- How is God's army described in Revelation 9:13–19? How does the devil's army compare to God's army?

  Revelation 9:13–19 contains a staggering description of God's army. It is numerically vast, consisting of two hundred million soldiers, which is ten times the population of the Roman Empire in the first century. The details of the army—breastplates of fire, sapphire, and sulfur; horses with heads like lions; tails like serpents—also communicate power and strength. Although the devil's army that is described in Revelation 9:7–10 is powerful and terrifying, the comparison between the armies reveals that God's army is greater.

- According to Revelation 9:20–21, how does the rest of humanity respond to the suffering and judgment that the wicked experience?

  Although Revelation 9 describes intense suffering experienced by unbelievers, the result of this suffering is not repentance but persistence in doing evil. The continuing sins described in these verses include sins against God—worship of demons and idols; they also include sins against one's neighbor—murder, sexual immorality, and theft.

Echoes of Ezekiel

- How does the third scene of the sixth trumpet refer the reader back to the book of Ezekiel?

  Revelation 10:8–11 describes a sequence of events in which John is told to take a scroll and eat it. Though sweet to the taste, it makes his stomach bitter. John is then told to prophesy on God's behalf. This sequence of events closely parallels Ezekiel's experience in Ezekiel 3:1–4. After this narrative, John is instructed to measure the temple in Revelation 11:1–2, a scene that evokes the detailed description of the measurements of a future temple in Ezekiel 40 and the following chapters.

- Is the temple described in Revelation 11 a physical building or a spiritual reality? Explain.

  Some interpreters view the temple described in Revelation 11:1–2 as a physical structure that will be rebuilt in Jerusalem in the future. However, Dr. Godfrey pointed out that this interpretation is not consistent with the way the temple is presented in the rest of Revelation. This book's approach so far is to envision the temple as a spiritual reality where the redeemed who belong to Christ worship the Lamb. Therefore, it is extremely unlikely that Revelation 11 would abruptly shift its focus to a physical temple.

After the Video

- How does Revelation 9 acknowledge the disheartening reality that, in spite of having access to God's truth, unbelievers so often persist in their unbelief?

  Revelation 9:20–21 describes the fact that, in spite of observing God's dramatic punishment of human wickedness, the unbelieving world continues to choose the path of sin without giving thought to repentance. This sad description of persistence in sin sounds familiar to many Christians who have tried repeatedly to share the gospel with friends and loved ones. Often believers feel at a loss to comprehend why certain unbelievers are so unreceptive to the gospel, yet Scripture describes this type of spiritual apathy as humanity's natural state apart from the regenerating work of the Holy Spirit.

- What is the difference between the big scroll of Revelation 5:1 and the little scroll of Revelation 10:2? What does this difference teach us about how God reveals His plans to us?

  The large scroll described in Revelation 5 represents the great events of history, the overarching story of redemption that God has revealed in Scripture. The smaller scroll represents the smaller-scale details that God has chosen not to reveal. Often, we desire to know the finer points of God's plan, such as what is going to happen tomorrow or what we should do in specific situations. Yet, God invites us instead to focus on His larger story and trust Him with the unknown details of our lives.

- How should we understand the reference to three and a half years in Revelation 11? How does this apply to the church's experience?

  The theme of three and a half years occurs frequently in redemptive history. In addition to the significance of the repeated nature of this number, three and a half also represents half of seven, which represents completion. Consequently, three and a half symbolizes a period of time that is cut short, a period that may seem long but is not really as long as it might have been. This number therefore hints at God's sovereignty and His perfect orchestration of the circumstances of His people.

REVIEW QUIZ

Lesson 11

1. **B.**
   The Nile in the south and Euphrates in the north formed the boundaries of the ancient Near East. The reference to one of these rivers in Revelation 9:14 signifies that these events occur in an important place but does not convey the universal scope that would have been understood if both of these rivers had been mentioned.

2. **C.**
   At most, the population of the entire Roman Empire at the time of John was twenty million. In contrast, the size of God's army recorded in Revelation 9:16 is twice ten thousand times ten thousand, or two hundred million. The idea being expressed is that the army of God is far greater than any human or demonic force.

3. **D.**
   God's army is described in Revelation 9:19 as having tails like the heads of serpents, imagery that communicates greater strength than the scorpion tails of the devil's army.

4. **C.**
   When the seven thunders sounded, John was about to record what they had said but was instructed not to do so. Although God has revealed a great deal of His plans and purposes to His church, some details will remain a mystery until Christ's return.

5. **A.**
   The large scroll in Revelation 5:1 was opened, revealing God's larger plan for human history. However, the smaller scroll described in 10:2 remains sealed, symbolizing God's plans and purposes that are not yet revealed.

6. **A.**
   Like the other references to a temple throughout Revelation, the description of a temple being measured in Revelation 11 refers to a heavenly, spiritual temple that includes God's people of all nations who are redeemed in Jesus Christ.

12

The Final Trumpets

INTRODUCTION

As we conclude our study of the third literary cycle in the book of Revelation, we encounter vivid descriptions of joyous celebration in heaven and of two witnesses who face opposition on earth. In Revelation 11, John continues to develop some of the major themes of this book, such as the faithful witness of God's people in the face of suffering, the world's refusal to repent and turn to Christ, and the culmination of Christ's rule over a new heaven and a new earth. In this lesson, Dr. Godfrey will examine this complex chapter and point out vital insights into God's work throughout history.

LEARNING GOALS

When you have finished this lesson, you should be able to:

- Describe the ministry and significance of the two witnesses in Revelation 11:3–13
- Summarize the meaning of the seventh trumpet in the third cycle of Revelation
- Articulate key themes of Revelation's third cycle

KEY IDEAS

- Christians are called to serve as God's witnesses to a world that does not know Him.
- Christians will face bitter opposition just as Jesus did during His earthly ministry.
- In spite of opposition, Christ's kingdom is present and triumphant.
- The real tragedy of human history is the refusal to repent and to believe.

REFLECTION & DISCUSSION QUESTIONS

Before the Video

What Do You Think?

Take a moment to answer the following questions. They will prepare you for the lecture.

- What does it mean to be a witness for Christ? What ideas does the word *witness* bring to mind?

- What are some Christian teachings that appeal to non-Christians? What are some Christian teachings that offend them?

Scripture Reading

And the angel who talked with me came again and woke me, like a man who is awakened out of his sleep. And he said to me, "What do you see?" I said, "I see, and behold, a lampstand all of gold, with a bowl on the top of it, and seven lamps on it, with seven lips on each of the lamps that are on the top of it. And there are two olive trees by it, one on the right of the bowl and the other on its left." And I said to the angel who talked with me, "What are these, my lord?" Then the angel who talked with me answered and said to me, "Do you not know what these are?" I said, "No, my lord." Then he said to me, "This is the word of the Lord *to Zerubbabel: Not by might, nor by power, but by my Spirit, says the* Lord *of hosts." . . . "These seven are the eyes of the* Lord*, which range through the whole earth." Then I said to him, "What are these two olive trees on the right and the left of the lampstand?" And a second time I answered and said to him, "What are these two branches of the olive trees, which are beside the two golden pipes from which the golden oil is poured out?" He said to me, "Do you not know what these are?" I said, "No, my lord." Then he said, "These are the two anointed ones who stand by the Lord of the whole earth."*

—Zechariah 4:1–6, 10b–14

- What similarities exist between this passage and the material covered so far in this study of Revelation?

During the Video

Answer the following questions while you watch the video. They will guide you through the lecture.

The Two Witnesses *0:00–15:37*

- What is the connection between Zechariah 4 and the two witnesses of Revelation 11:3–12?

- How is the city identified in Revelation 11:8? What truth does this reveal?

The Seventh Trumpet *15:37–23:22*

- How is the statement in Revelation 11:15, "The kingdom of the world has become the kingdom of our Lord and of his Christ," best interpreted?

- In what way is the celebration of God's people in heaven also considered a woe to some?

After the Video

Answer the following questions after you have finished the lecture. They will help you identify and summarize the major points.

- How does Revelation 11 present chronological parallels between the church and the life of Christ? What basic message do these parallels convey?

  If you are in a group, have the members read John 15:18–21. What do you find troubling in these verses? What in these verses gives you hope?

- What does the reaction of the people to the killing of the witnesses say about the world's tolerance for hearing truth? How do we see this same principle at work in our culture?

  If you are in a group, have the members read 2 Timothy 4:3–4. How does our culture behave in the way that is described in these verses? In what ways are Christians tempted to do this as well?

- According to Dr. Godfrey, is it accurate to describe present-day Jerusalem as a holy city? Do you agree or disagree? Explain your answer.

  If you are in a group, have the members discuss what it means for any city or place to be considered holy. Where is true holiness found? How do we experience it? What would make a place holy?

PRAYER

Commit what you have learned from God's Word in this lesson to prayer.

- Praise God for establishing a kingdom in Christ that shall have no end.
- Confess any rival kingdoms that compete for your allegiance.
- Thank God for His faithful witnesses who have proclaimed the truth in all ages.
- Ask God to help you represent Christ with boldness and humility.

REVIEW QUIZ

Use these multiple-choice questions to measure what you learned from this lesson.

1. The account of the two witnesses in Revelation 11:3–12 evokes imagery associated with which two Old Testament figures?
   a. Balak and Balaam
   b. David and Solomon
   c. Jacob and Esau
   d. Moses and Elijah
2. Which of the following best describes the identity of the two witnesses?
   a. Church
   b. Enoch and Elijah
   c. First-century Apostles
   d. Unknown future prophets
3. All *except* which of the following are parallels between the two witnesses and Jesus?
   a. Ascension to heaven in a cloud
   b. Burial
   c. Completion of their mission
   d. Resurrection
4. The physical city of Jerusalem remains an objectively holy city today.
   a. True
   b. False
5. What future holy site does the book of Revelation anticipate?
   a. Heaven
   b. Jerusalem
   c. New heaven and new earth
   d. Strictly speaking, no site shall be considered holy again.
6. Which of the following best describes the Christian's posture toward the arrival of the kingdom?
   a. Waiting for Christ's millennial kingdom to appear
   b. Waiting for a future kingdom to be established
   c. Waiting for the present kingdom to be revealed
   d. Working to create the kingdom now

Answer Key—The Final Trumpets

REFLECTION & DISCUSSION QUESTIONS

Before the Video

What Do You Think?

These are personal questions. The answers should be based on your own knowledge and experience.

Scripture Reading

- What similarities exist between this passage and the material covered so far in this study of Revelation?

  Zechariah 4 exhibits symbolic features that are very similar to parts of Revelation. Both passages describe visions of God's heavenly temple. In both instances, seven gold lampstands are mentioned. In Zechariah, they symbolize the eyes of the Lord, which range through the whole earth. In Revelation, the lampstands represent the seven churches upon which God's watchful eyes rest. Both Zechariah and Revelation refer to two anointed figures appointed by God to bear witness to God's mighty deeds. Both are also written to offer hope to God's people in times of uncertainty. As Zechariah 4:6 indicates, true hope is found not in human might or power but in the Spirit of the Lord.

During the Video

The Two Witnesses

- What is the connection between Zechariah 4 and the two witnesses of Revelation 11:3–12?

  Revelation 11:4 identifies the two witnesses with "the two olive trees and the two lampstands that stand before the Lord of the earth." This statement alludes to Zechariah 4, where the lampstands in the temple of God never run out of oil because there is a direct flow of oil from the olive trees into the lampstands. This allusion indicates that the two witnesses of Revelation 11 will never run out of the oil that allows them to testify to Christ because Christ Himself provides the oil that will forever replenish their faithful witness.

- How is the city identified in Revelation 11:8? What truth does this reveal?

  The city where the two witnesses prophesy and are eventually put to death is described as the city where Jesus was crucified and as "the great city that symbolically is called Sodom and Egypt." Throughout the rest of Revelation, the phrase "great city" is associated with Babylon. Among other things, these references indicate that the earthly city Jerusalem no longer functions as God's holy city. Instead, the holy city is now found in heaven and will one day be made manifest in the new Jerusalem. In the meantime, the earthly Jerusalem has become subject to the same spiritual maladies as other earthly cities such as Sodom or Babylon.

The Seventh Trumpet

- How is the statement in Revelation 11:15, "The kingdom of the world has become the kingdom of our Lord and of his Christ," best interpreted?

  Some have interpreted this statement in a way that seems to equate Christ's kingdom with particular earthly nations and governments. However, this statement is more accurately understood to indicate Christ's lordship over every nation and all human affairs. This verse shows that Christ has already begun to reign. The ascended Christ is even now King of kings and Lord of lords.

- In what way is the celebration of God's people in heaven also considered a woe to some?

  Dr. Godfrey points out that the victory of God's people is also a woe to the wicked who will not believe. Exodus 15:11–16 expresses this contrast between the rejoicing of God's rescued people and the dismay of the unbelieving nations. Scripture anticipates the eschatological reality that those who have rejected Christ will one day behold the rejoicing of God's people but will sadly be unable to enter that rejoicing because of their unbelief.

After the Video

- How does Revelation 11 present chronological parallels between the church and the life of Christ? What basic message do these parallels convey?

  The account of the two witnesses, who are symbolic of the church, contains many parallels to the life of Christ. These parallels include the finishing or completion of their work, their death, the period of three days after their death, their resurrection, and their ascension to heaven on a cloud. These vivid parallels convey the message that we, as servants of Christ, will walk the same path that the Master walked. As a result of our union with Him, we will face opposition, we will die with Him, and we will be raised with Him.

- What does the reaction of the people to the killing of the witnesses say about the world's tolerance for hearing truth? How do we see this same principle at work in our culture?

  Revelation 11:7–10 reveals that the inhabitants of the city do not behold the killing of the two witnesses and allow their bodies to lie in the street, but they also consider the death of the witnesses to be a cause of celebration. Verse 10 describes the testimony of the witnesses as a torment to the unbelievers, who will then proceed to make merry and exchange gifts in celebration of their demise. This reaction indicates that to many unbelievers, the mere experience of being told the truth amounts to torment. Tolerance for truth is low in our culture, which places a premium on individual autonomy and pleasure.

- According to Dr. Godfrey, is it accurate to describe present-day Jerusalem as a holy city? Do you agree or disagree? Explain your answer.

  Dr. Godfrey points out that the present-day city of Jerusalem is a significant place that is well worth visiting and learning about. Yet, strictly speaking, it is not a holy city. For centuries, God focused His redemptive work on one people, one land, and one city. With the coming of Jesus, God's redemptive focus has expanded from Jerusalem to Judea and Samaria and to the ends of the earth. Once, Jerusalem was the place where God's glory dwelled in the physical temple. Now, believers are the new temple where God's Spirit resides. Christians await the day when the whole world will be renewed and God will create a new holy land with a new Jerusalem. Until then, no one place on earth is any more or less holy than any other.

REVIEW QUIZ

Lesson 12

1. **D.**
   Key features and descriptions of the two witnesses—such as their power to prevent rainfall, to turn water into blood, to strike the earth with plagues, and to call down fire from heaven—evoke memorable events from the lives of Moses and Elijah. This description of the witnesses presents a synopsis of the whole history of God's revelatory work through His prophets and preachers.

2. **A.**
   The account of the two witnesses in Revelation 11 presents a symbolic description of the testimony of the church in the midst of a hostile and unbelieving world.

3. **B.**
   Parallels between the witnesses and the life of Christ include completion of their work, death at the hands of others, resurrection, and ascension to heaven. A difference between the account of the witnesses and the life of Christ is the fact that Jesus was buried in a tomb but the witnesses are not; instead, their bodies lie in the street for three and a half days until God raises them from the dead.

4. **B.**
   While Jerusalem is of vital significance throughout redemptive history as a geographic focal point of God's redemptive work, it is no longer a holy city. The Spirit of the Lord no longer dwells in an earthly temple but dwells instead in the hearts of believers, who form part of God's spiritual, heavenly temple. Because God's redemptive focus now extends to the ends of the earth, Jerusalem is not any more or less holy than any other city.

5. **C.**
   Revelation, affirming that the whole world belongs to God, looks ahead to the restoration of all things and the creation of a new heaven and a new earth.

6. **C.**
   Dr. Godfrey pointed out that because Christ is reigning now, Christians are not in a state of waiting for a future kingdom. Nor do they face the pressure of bringing in the kingdom through their own efforts. Rather, Christians can celebrate the fact that the kingdom is already present and will be fully revealed when Christ returns.

13

The Woman & the Dragon

INTRODUCTION

After presenting the first three literary cycles of seven letters, seven seals, and seven trumpets, John unveils a dramatic narrative about a woman and a dragon. Depicting the devil's ferocious onslaught against the people of God, this central cycle of Revelation offers a vivid account of the trials and tribulations that Christians experience on earth. Nevertheless, this account also offers God's people encouragement and hope that the dragon is defeated and their victory is assured.

LEARNING GOALS

When you have finished this lesson, you should be able to:

- Describe the literary structure and major themes of the fourth cycle of Revelation
- Articulate a sound biblical view of spiritual warfare

KEY IDEAS

- Satan has been cast out of heaven, and his power has been broken.
- Though he has been defeated, the devil is still a dangerous spiritual opponent.
- God has extended His protection over His church and has limited its time of hardship.
- Despite bitter opposition, Christians will emerge victorious from their spiritual battles.

REFLECTION & DISCUSSION QUESTIONS

Before the Video

What Do You Think?

Take a moment to answer the following questions. They will prepare you for the lecture.

- What role does spiritual warfare play in the lives of Christians today?

- What weapons and tactics does Satan use against Christians in spiritual warfare? What kind of spiritual attacks are most successful?

Scripture Reading

And I heard a loud voice in heaven, saying, "Now the salvation and the power and the kingdom of our God and the authority of his Christ have come, for the accuser of our brothers has been thrown down, who accuses them day and night before our God. And they have conquered him by the blood of the Lamb and by the word of their testimony, for they loved not their lives even unto death. Therefore, rejoice, O heavens and you who dwell in them! But woe to you, O earth and sea, for the devil has come down to you in great wrath, because he knows that his time is short!"

—Revelation 12:10–12

- What do these verses say about the devil's status? What strategy does he use against believers? How do Christians overcome his attacks?

During the Video

Answer the following questions while you watch the video. They will guide you through the lecture.

The First and Second Visions *0:00–15:39*

- Why is the reference to the ark of the covenant in Revelation 11:19 surprising? What is the connection between the ark of the covenant and Jesus?

- What role do chiasms play in the fourth cycle of the book of Revelation?

- Does the woman in Revelation 12 represent the Virgin Mary or someone else? Explain.

The Third and Fourth Visions *15:39–25:11*

- What two levels of existence does the casting out of Satan from heaven imply?

- In what sense is Revelation 12:13–17 the heart of the book of Revelation?

After the Video

Answer the following questions after you have finished the lecture. They will help you identify and summarize the major points.

- In Revelation 12, what is the relationship between the spiritual conflict in heaven and the conflict that Christians experience on earth?

  If you are in a group, have the members read Job 1:6–12 and Job 2:1–13. How do these passages reveal two levels of spiritual conflict?

- Against whom does the dragon fight? What does this reveal about the nature of spiritual warfare?

  If you are in a group, have the members describe their own experiences with spiritual warfare. How have you personally experienced the enemy's attacks? How has God given you victory against the enemy?

- What is the significance of the period of three and a half years in Revelation 12?

  If you are in a group, have the members discuss a time of spiritual hardship that they have endured. How long did this hardship last? How did God reveal his timing in the midst of this difficulty or struggle?

PRAYER

Commit what you have learned from God's Word in this lesson to prayer.

- Praise God for casting Satan out of heaven and limiting his power.
- Confess ways that you fall prey to the devil's accusations.
- Thank God for giving you strength to withstand the devil's onslaught.
- Ask God to help you overcome the devil's schemes through the blood of the Lamb and the word of your testimony.

REVIEW QUIZ

Use these multiple-choice questions to measure what you learned from this lesson.

1. What is the topic of the first and seventh visions of Revelation's fourth cycle?
   a. Beasts
   b. Church
   c. Prophets
   d. War
2. Which theme forms a parallel between the beginning of the book of Job and the second vision of Revelation's fourth cycle?
   a. Earthly conflict rooted in heavenly conflict
   b. Meaningless suffering
   c. Seasons of trial in the wilderness
   d. Testing of the righteous
3. According to Revelation 12:6, what is the duration of the church's period of exile and suffering?
   a. 40 days and nights
   b. 1,260 days
   c. 1,000 years
   d. 7 years
4. What is the topic of the second and sixth visions of Revelation's fourth cycle?
   a. Beasts
   b. Church
   c. Prophets
   d. War
5. John uses all *except* which of the following to describe the dragon in Revelation 12:9?
   a. Ancient serpent
   b. Devil
   c. Lucifer
   d. Satan
6. What is the topic of the third and fifth visions of Revelation's fourth cycle?
   a. Celebration
   b. Church
   c. Plagues
   d. War

Answer Key—The Woman & the Dragon

REFLECTION & DISCUSSION QUESTIONS

Before the Video

What Do You Think?

These are personal questions. The answers should be based on your own knowledge and experience.

Scripture Reading

- What do these verses say about the devil's status? What strategy does he use against believers? How do Christians overcome his attacks?

  These verses proclaim that the devil, or the accuser, has been thrown down. As a result, he lashes out against the earth in great wrath because he knows that his days are short. Verse 10 indicates that he uses the strategy of accusation against believers, accusing them day and night before God. In spite of such fierce accusation, believers shall overcome by the blood of the Lamb and by the word of their testimony.

During the Video

The First and Second Visions

- Why is the reference to the ark of the covenant in Revelation 11:19 surprising? What is the connection between the ark of the covenant and Jesus?

  The reference to the ark of the covenant in Revelation 11:19 would have been striking to John's original audience, not just because the ark had disappeared several centuries earlier, but also because it had never been publicly seen by the people of Israel. Nevertheless, Revelation 11:19 presents the temple as open with the ark visible to all. Because the physical ark had faded from redemptive history, the reference to the ark in this passage likely points to Jesus. The original ark had contained the law, which Jesus fulfilled. It also contained the rod of Aaron, which budded in representation of resurrection. Additionally, it had included the jar of manna, which prefigured Jesus as the true bread of heaven. Moreover, just as the ark had a mercy seat, Jesus is the mercy seat for sinners. Therefore, Jesus Christ represents the ultimate fulfillment of the ark of the covenant.

- What role do chiasms play in the fourth cycle of the book of Revelation?

  Dr. Godfrey observes that literary chiasms form both the overall structure of Revelation and the structure of the fourth and central cycle of the book. The outer layer, consisting of the first and seventh visions, describes the church. Next, the second and sixth visions describe true and false prophets. The third and fifth visions, in turn, describe war. Finally, the fourth and central vision describes the history of the church, which is one of the dominant themes of the book as a whole.

- Does the woman in Revelation 12 represent the Virgin Mary or someone else? Explain.

  Although the Virgin Mary is often portrayed with symbolism that appears in Revelation 12, Dr. Godfrey argues that the woman presented in this chapter is better understood as the church. Although Mary was pregnant and gave birth to Jesus, as presented in this passage, it can also rightly be said that Jesus is the son and heir of the Old Testament people of God, symbolized by the woman. Moreover, other imagery from this passage—such as the woman's flight from the dragon, her sojourn in the wilderness, and her experiences of persecution—is not true of Mary but is true of the church.

The Third and Fourth Visions

- What two levels of existence does the casting out of Satan from heaven imply?

  Dr. Godfrey points out that the references to the dragon's being cast down from heaven in Revelation 12:9 and 12:13 highlight two distinct levels of existence. First is the heavenly realm where God reigns, where Christ is enthroned, and where the angelic host and the redeemed of humanity worship Him. Second is the earth, where Satan has been cast down, where those who dwell on earth live in opposition to God, and where God's people are called to persevere in the face of temporary but violent opposition.

- In what sense is Revelation 12:13–17 the heart of the book of Revelation?

  Revelation 12:13–17 forms the fourth and central vision in the fourth and central cycle of the book of Revelation. Therefore, this passage appears directly at the structural center of the book. Moreover, its content, which deals with the dragon's unsuccessful attempts to destroy the woman, summarizes the dominant theme of Revelation, the church's persistence in faithfulness in spite of opposition and spiritual warfare.

After the Video

- In Revelation 12, what is the relationship between the spiritual conflict in heaven and the conflict that Christians experience on earth?

  Revelation 12 presents an account of spiritual warfare that takes place on both a heavenly level and an earthly level. Verses 7–10 describe Satan's defeat in the heavenly realm and his exile to earth. Verses 13–17 depict his furious but unsuccessful onslaught against the woman and her offspring on earth. This chapter reveals that the intense spiritual opposition that Christians experience is carried out by an enemy who has already been defeated but is still dangerous. Nevertheless, Christians are assured that Satan's attacks against them will not succeed and that his final defeat is certain.

- Against whom does the dragon fight? What does this reveal about the nature of spiritual warfare?

  Revelation 12:7 describes a spiritual war that is fought between Michael and other angels against the dragon. God Himself does not fight the dragon; the power of the angels is enough to rout Satan and cast him and his angels from heaven. This passage reveals the vital truth that God's power is vastly greater than Satan's power. In our struggles against Satan and his minions, Christians can have confidence that we are on the victorious side.

- What is the significance of the period of three and a half years in Revelation 12?

  Revelation 12 mentions a period of three and a half years in verses 6 and 14. The first reference describes this period as 1,260 days, in which the woman has fled to the wilderness to be nourished in a place prepared by God. The second reference to "a time, and times, and half a time" describes the same period of nourishment in the wilderness. This duration of time, representing half of seven, or a period of time that has been cut short by God, symbolizes the church's season of awaiting Christ's return. Although this period of time seems to be long, it is, in fact, a shortened duration of time.

REVIEW QUIZ

Lesson 13

1. **B.**
   The first and seventh visions of Revelation's central cycle, which form the outer layer of this cycle's chiasm, present descriptions of the church.

2. **A.**
   Revelation 12 and Job 1–2 both illustrate the principle that spiritual conflict in heaven forms the backdrop for spiritual conflict on earth. Christians can take heart in the knowledge that their struggles are part of a larger spiritual war in which God is victorious.

3. **B.**
   Revelation 12:6 identifies the church's period of suffering as 1,260 days. This number, approximately half of seven years, symbolizes a duration of time that God has limited.

4. **C.**
   Dr. Godfrey points out that the second and sixth visions describe prophets. The second vision portrays the true prophet, and the sixth vision depicts Satan's counterfeit prophet. The topic of the first and seventh visions of Revelation 12 is the church.

5. **C.**
   Revelation 12:9 describes the dragon as "that ancient serpent, who is called the devil and Satan, the deceiver of the whole world." The name Lucifer does not appear in this passage.

6. **D.**
   The third and fifth visions portray scenes of war. In the third vision, the dragon is cast down. In the fifth vision, he unsuccessfully attempts to wage war against God's forces. The topic of the first and seventh visions of Revelation 12 is the church, and the topic of the second and sixth visions is prophets.

14

The Two Beasts

INTRODUCTION

In one of the most famous sections of the book of Revelation, John imparts a vision of the great dragon, Satan, looming by the side of the sea and summoning forth a powerful beast to wage war against God's people. To reinforce this beast's power, a second beast emerges from the earth and seeks to persuade all people to worship the first beast. This unholy trinity, which dominates the central literary cycle of Revelation, has prompted debate, discussion, and speculation among interpreters for centuries. In this lesson, Dr. Godfrey will examine this vivid passage and reveal its message of practical insight and unwavering hope: try as they may, Satan and his beasts cannot and will not defeat God's people.

LEARNING GOALS

When you have finished this lesson, you should be able to:

- Summarize the message of visions four, five, and six of Revelation's fourth literary cycle
- Identify and describe the characters who make up the devil's unholy trinity
- Articulate why Christians do not need to live in fear of the devil and his forces

KEY IDEAS

- Thwarted in his efforts to destroy the church, Satan targets individual believers.
- Satan counterfeits the things of God—even the Trinity itself—in an effort to deceive humanity.
- In every way, there's a satanic effort to deceive true believers. In every way, it will fail.

REFLECTION & DISCUSSION QUESTIONS

Before the Video

What Do You Think?

Take a moment to answer the following questions. They will prepare you for the lecture.

- What are some ways that people try to imitate God? What are ways that Satan tries to imitate God?

- What have you been taught about the beast in Revelation 13? How do most Christians view the identity and significance of the beast?

Scripture Reading

And when the dragon saw that he had been thrown down to the earth, he pursued the woman who had given birth to the male child. But the woman was given the two wings of the great eagle so that she might fly from the serpent into the wilderness, to the place where she is to be nourished for a time, and times, and half a time. The serpent poured water like a river out of his mouth after the woman, to sweep her away with a flood. But the earth came to the help of the woman, and the earth opened its mouth and swallowed the river that the dragon had poured from his mouth. Then the dragon became furious with the woman and went off to make war on the rest of her offspring, on those who keep the commandments of God and hold to the testimony of Jesus. And he stood on the sand of the sea.

—Revelation 12:13–17

- What are some of the ways in this passage that Satan attempts to defeat the woman and her offspring? How successful is he?

During the Video

Answer the following questions while you watch the video. They will guide you through the lecture.

The Fourth Vision *0:00–4:57*

- How does Dr. Godfrey describe the church's time in the wilderness?

- What is the worst damage that the devil can inflict on God's people?

The Fifth Vision *4:57–17:47*

- According to Dr. Godfrey, what type of power does the beast from the sea represent?

- How do the forty-two months of the beast's authority line up chronologically with the forty-two months of the woman's nourishment?

The Sixth Vision *17:47–24:39*

- In what way does the second beast attempt to imitate God?

- What unique feature of the image of the beast is mentioned in Revelation 13:15? How do accounts of ancient history describe similar phenomena?

After the Video

Answer the following questions after you have finished the lecture. They will help you identify and summarize the major points.

- What is the significance of the dragon standing by the sea in Revelation 12:17?

  If you are in a group, have the members discuss ways that Satan can use chaos, confusion, or disorder as a spiritual attack. How have you seen God bring order out of chaos?

- How does Revelation's fourth cycle describe ways that Satan attempts to imitate or counterfeit God? What message emerges from this pattern?

  If you are in a group, have the members share examples of poor imitations that they have encountered. How does the fourth cycle's presentation of Satan's poor imitations of God offer encouragement to Christians?

- Read Revelation 13:10. What is the translation difference that Dr. Godfrey points out? What difference does this wording make?

  If you are in a group, have the members describe a time when God's promises gave them hope and strength to withstand hardship.

PRAYER

Commit what you have learned from God's Word in this lesson to prayer.

- Praise God for His surpassing greatness above rival gods and Satan's counterfeit trinity.
- Confess any doubts you may have about God's ability or faithfulness to sustain you in the wilderness.
- Thank God for sustaining His church in its period of exile in the wilderness.
- Ask God for the spiritual nourishment you need to withstand the devil's spiritual attacks.

REVIEW QUIZ

Use these multiple-choice questions to measure what you learned from this lesson.

1. Which of the following represents the worst damage Satan can do to the people of God?
   a. Accusation
   b. Loss of faith
   c. Martyrdom
   d. Persecution
2. What did the sea primarily represent to the ancient Israelites?
   a. Chaos
   b. Exploration
   c. Livelihood
   d. Salvation
3. The first beast's wound represents a satanic imitation of which of the following?
   a. Baptism
   b. Incarnation
   c. Regeneration
   d. Resurrection
4. Only those whose names are not written in the Book of Life will worship the beast.
   a. True
   b. False
5. The second beast's work represents a satanic imitation of which of the following?
   a. Inspiration
   b. Incarnation
   c. Regeneration
   d. Resurrection
6. The mark of the beast represents a satanic imitation of which of the following?
   a. Baptism
   b. Communion
   c. Incarnation
   d. Prophecy

Answer Key—The Two Beasts

REFLECTION & DISCUSSION QUESTIONS

Before the Video

What Do You Think?

These are personal questions. The answers should be based on your own knowledge and experience.

Scripture Reading

- What are some of the ways in this passage that Satan attempts to defeat the woman and her offspring? How successful is he?

  These verses describe three of Satan's attempts to defeat the woman and her offspring. First, he pursues the woman until she is given two wings to escape into the wilderness. Next, he attempts to leverage the forces of nature to sweep her away, but the earth itself comes to her aid. Finally, Satan abandons his attacks against the woman and attempts to make war on her children. Despite his persistent efforts, Satan ultimately fails to defeat the woman and her offspring.

During the Video

The Fourth Vision

- How does Dr. Godfrey describe the church's time in the wilderness?

  Revelation 12:6 and 12:14 refer to the church's flight into the wilderness, where she receives God's nourishment amid the fury of the dragon. This picture of the church is consistent with the New Testament witness that Christians are experiencing a period of temporary exile until Christ's return. Dr. Godfrey also used an Old Testament metaphor that the church is like Israel in the wilderness on the way to the promised land but not yet there. Although we are presently in the wilderness, God is nevertheless sustaining us and preserving us so that we will emerge from our exile when the appointed time has run its course.

- What is the worst damage that the devil can inflict on God's people?

  Revelation 12:17 reports that the devil, furious over his failure to destroy the woman, has settled for waging war on the rest of her children. Unable to defeat the church, Satan's strategy has become to destroy as many individual Christians as he can. Yet, Dr. Godfrey pointed out that the devil's power is so limited that the worst he can do is kill us and send us to heaven. The fact that the maximum harm the devil can inflict on God's elect is to send them to glory illustrates how utterly defeated he is.

The Fifth Vision

- According to Dr. Godfrey, what type of power does the beast from the sea represent?

  Although some commentators view the beast from the sea as a representative of political power, Dr. Godfrey contends that the beast instead represents religious power. While political power is an important topic in the book of Revelation, Dr. Godfrey notes that false religion often undergirds oppressive political power.

- How do the forty-two months of the beast's authority line up chronologically with the forty-two months of the woman's nourishment?

  Revelation 13:5 reports that the beast is allowed to exercise authority for forty-two months. This is the same duration of time, three and a half years, as the woman's period of nourishment in the wilderness described in Revelation 12:6, 14. Although some commentators believe that these periods of three and a half years occur sequentially, Dr. Godfrey argues that these time periods are concurrent, describing the same period of time with differing emphases on the role of the dragon, beast, and woman.

The Sixth Vision

- In what way does the second beast attempt to imitate God?

  The second beast, which rose from out of the earth and is described in Revelation 13:11–18, performs signs and wonders in order to persuade the inhabitants of the earth to worship the first beast. This second beast represents Satan's imitation of the Holy Spirit, who bears testimony to Jesus.

- What unique feature of the image of the beast is mentioned in Revelation 13:15? How do accounts of ancient history describe similar phenomena?

  Revelation 13:15 mentions that the beast's prophet was allowed to give breath to the image of the beast so that it might speak. Though the precise meaning of this description is unclear, John may be envisioning a scenario that is similar to ancient temples where images of false gods were engineered in such a way that the priest could secretly move the image's jaws and speak through the image.

After the Video

- What is the significance of the dragon standing by the sea in Revelation 12:17?

  God's people in the ancient world considered the sea dangerous, unpredictable, and chaotic. Consequently, the presentation of the dragon standing by the sea communicates the idea that he is communing with the forces of chaos and destruction in order to wage war against the people of God.

- How does Revelation's fourth cycle describe ways that Satan attempts to imitate or counterfeit God? What message emerges from this pattern?

In Revelation's fourth cycle, Satan attempts to imitate God in a variety of ways. First is his unsuccessful attempt in 12:15–16 to marshal the forces of nature against the church. Next is his act of summoning a beast from the sea to do his bidding, as an imitation of the Father's sending the Son to earth. The beast from the sea, with its mortal wound that has healed, represents an imitation of Christ's death and resurrection. Moreover, the beast from the land, which leads the inhabitants of earth to worship the first beast, represents an imitation of the Holy Spirit, who leads unbelievers to Christ. Although this counterfeit Trinity attempts to lead believers astray, it will ultimately fail to undermine the faith of the people of God.

- Read Revelation 13:10. What is the translation difference that Dr. Godfrey points out? What difference does this wording make?

  Dr. Godfrey points out that the ESV concludes Revelation 13:10 with the statement "Here is a call for the endurance and faith of the saints." He also points out that the words "a call" do not appear in the original Greek. In the ESV reading, God is appealing to His saints to persevere and have faith, but the outcome rests ultimately on them. In the Greek reading, "Here is the endurance and faith of the saints," God is extending His guarantee to preserve His people. Therefore, the focus of this verse is not on us and our deeds but on God and His deeds. The greater our difficulty, the more important it is to be surrounded by God's promises.

REVIEW QUIZ

Lesson 14

1. **C.**
   Although Satan is the accuser of Christians and incites his followers to oppose and persecute believers, he is powerless to snatch Christians out of Christ's hand. The worst damage he can inflict on God's people is to kill them, which results in their glorious arrival in heaven.

2. **A.**
   To the ancient people of Israel, the sea represented chaos and fear. Consequently, the appearance of the dragon standing next to the sea in Revelation 12:17 signals Satan's alliance with the forces of chaos and destruction.

3. **D.**
   The beast that appears from the sea bears a mortal wound that has healed. Within the devil's unholy trinity, this wound represents the "resurrection" of the counterfeit Christ.

4. **A.**
   Revelation 13:8 records that "all who dwell on earth will worship it, everyone whose name has not been written before the foundation of the world in the book of life of the Lamb who was slain."

5. **C.**
   The second beast's primary role is to lead the inhabitants of the earth to worship the first beast. Within the devil's unholy trinity, the second beast represents a counterfeit version of the Holy Spirit's work of regeneration, awakening those who are spiritually dead to come to Christ.

6. **A.**
   The mark of the beast, applied to the right hand or forehead of all who serve the beast, functions as a sign and seal of the devil's false religion. This sign given to the beast's followers represents a satanic imitation of the sacrament of baptism, which marks those who are included in God's covenant community.

15

The Mark & the Call to Endure

INTRODUCTION

No matter how fiercely Satan may attempt to subdue God's people, his efforts will end in failure. This principle is powerfully seen at the end of Revelation's fourth cycle, with its description of the mark of the beast and the final victory of God's people. As the focus of John's visions begins to shift from the church's perseverance to the judgment that awaits the wicked, the pastoral thrust of John's message remains the same: repent and persevere.

LEARNING GOALS

When you have finished this lesson, you should be able to:

- Summarize the message of visions six and seven of Revelation's fourth literary cycle
- Describe the structure and message of Revelation's fifth literary cycle
- Articulate an informed perspective on major themes such as the mark of the beast and Babylon the Great

KEY IDEAS

- Rather than incite fear among the Christians, the mark of the beast demonstrates God's victory over Satan.
- Although the church will have many struggles, Christ will triumph in and for His people.
- When God's judgment falls on the wicked, earthly powers will be overturned, but God's people will experience blessing, triumph, and rest.

REFLECTION & DISCUSSION QUESTIONS

Before the Video

What Do You Think?

Take a moment to answer the following questions. They will prepare you for the lecture.

- What pictures or ideas does the number 666 evoke? How have you seen this number presented in the church or in popular culture?
- Why is Babylon important in the Bible? What does Babylon have to do with the book of Revelation?

Scripture Reading

Then I saw another angel flying directly overhead, with an eternal gospel to proclaim to those who dwell on earth, to every nation and tribe and language and people. And he said with a loud voice, "Fear God and give him glory, because the hour of his judgment has come, and worship him who made heaven and earth, the sea and the springs of water."

—Revelation 14:6–7

- To whom is the angel in Revelation 14:6–7 sent? What does this angel call people to do? Why should they do this?

During the Video

Answer the following questions while you watch the video. They will guide you through the lecture.

The Mark of the Beast *0:00–6:01*

- Why does Dr. Godfrey argue that the identity of the beast is neither a secret nor a prophecy of a future person at the end of history?
- What is gematria? How has this technique been used to try to identify the beast?

The Seventh Vision *6:01–11:32*

- Is Revelation 14:4 an argument for Christians not to marry? Explain.

- What is the overall blessing communicated in the fourth cycle of Revelation?

Three Angelic Appearances *11:32–25:44*

- What is the literary relationship between Revelation's third and fifth cycles?

- According to Revelation 14:12–13, what is the application for Christians after hearing the warnings of judgment issued to nonbelievers?

After the Video

Answer the following questions after you have finished the lecture. They will help you identify and summarize the major points.

- According to Dr. Godfrey, what does the number 666 actually mean? How does this meaning offer encouragement to Christians?

  If you are in a group, have the members discuss the summary of the mark of the beast in this lesson and the previous lesson. What do you think of Dr. Godfrey's explanation of the mark and of the number 666? How does his view differ from other teachings you have heard?

- What picture of the church emerges from Revelation's fourth literary cycle? What kind of progression is described?

  If you are in a group, have the members describe moments when the church has appeared to be weak and moments when it has appeared to be strong.

- What does Babylon represent? How is Babylon introduced in the book of Revelation? Why is this significant?

  If you are in a group, have the members reflect on the role that Babylon plays in today's world. How is Babylon's influence at work in contemporary culture?

PRAYER

Commit what you have learned from God's Word in this lesson to prayer.

- Praise God for His sovereignty in judgment, in mercy, and over all of human history.
- Confess ways that you are prone to discouragement or tempted to give up hope.
- Thank God for clearly communicating His victory and ours throughout Revelation.
- Ask God to increase your faith, that you would rejoice even in your sufferings.

REVIEW QUIZ

Use these multiple-choice questions to measure what you learned from this lesson.

1. The term *gematria* best describes which of the following?
   a. Assigning numerical values to letters and adding up numbers for certain words
   b. Finding parallels between ancient prophecies and historical events
   c. Solving literary riddles or word puzzles
   d. Studying ancient texts to determine their contemporary meaning

2. Which of the following best describes the theme of the seventh vision in Revelation's fourth cycle?
   a. The battle between God and Satan
   b. The beast's war against Christians
   c. The church's struggle
   d. The church's triumph

3. Which of the following best describes the meaning of "blameless" in Revelation 14:5?
   a. Covenantally faithful
   b. Morally innocent
   c. Morally perfect
   d. Sinless

4. The literary structure of Revelation's fifth cycle is formed by the appearances of seven angels.
   a. True
   b. False

5. When judgment comes in Revelation, it does not come on those who never had a chance to respond.
   a. True
   b. False

6. What kind of power did Babylon primarily represent in the ancient world?
   a. Cultural influence
   b. Lucrative trade routes
   c. Military might
   d. Religious power

Answer Key—
The Mark & the Call to Endure

REFLECTION & DISCUSSION QUESTIONS

Before the Video

What Do You Think?

These are personal questions. The answers should be based on your own knowledge and experience.

Scripture Reading

- To whom is the angel in Revelation 14:6–7 sent? What does this angel call people to do? Why should they do this?

  The angel described in these verses goes forth with a message for those who dwell on earth, to every nation and tribe and language and people. This angel urges the inhabitants of earth to fear God and give Him glory. The basis for this call to fear God is twofold: (1) because God is Creator of all things, His creatures ought to honor and glorify Him; (2) because the hour of judgment is at hand, people are urged to turn to God while there is still time.

During the Video

The Mark of the Beast

- Why does Dr. Godfrey argue that the identity of the beast is neither a secret nor a prophecy of a future person at the end of history?

  In reference to the mark of the beast, Revelation 13:18 says, "This calls for wisdom: let the one who has understanding calculate the number of the beast." This statement indicates that the number of the beast is a truth that is accessible to any Christian who possesses wisdom and understanding. Moreover, this number must also be something that first-century Christians could figure out. Consequently, it refers neither to a secret nor to a person born centuries later. Rather, the ordinary Christians who read this letter in John's day would have been able to figure out who the beast was.

- What is gematria? How has this technique been used to try to identify the beast?

  Gematria is an alphanumeric system in which numerical values are assigned to letters. Throughout history, Bible commentators have often tried to use gematria to determine the identity of the beast by finding names whose Greek numerical values add up to 666. Although this approach has tempted many commentators,

Dr. Godfrey pointed out that the practice of gematria does not appear anywhere else in Revelation and is therefore unlikely to be the key to understanding the mark of the beast.

The Seventh Vision

- Is Revelation 14:4 an argument for Christians not to marry? Explain.

  The reference in Revelation 14:4 to the 144,000 redeemed as those "who have not defiled themselves with women, for they are virgins" appears on the surface to be an exhortation not to marry. However, Dr. Godfrey argued that this verse is best understood in light of 2 Corinthians 11:2, where Paul expresses his desire to present the Corinthian believers to Christ "as a pure virgin." In a similar way, Revelation 14:4 exhorts Christians to maintain their spiritual virginity by remaining faithful to Christ instead of committing spiritual adultery with idols.

- What is the overall blessing communicated in the fourth cycle of Revelation?

  The fourth cycle of Revelation, which begins with a struggle between the woman and the dragon and ends with the saints in victory, communicates the overall blessing that although the church will have many struggles, Christ will triumph in and for His people.

Three Angelic Appearances

- What is the literary relationship between Revelation's third and fifth cycles?

  Due to the chiastic arrangement of Revelation's seven literary cycles, the third cycle corresponds to the fifth cycle. Both of these cycles deal with the topic of suffering; the third cycle focused on the suffering of the wicked in history, and the fifth cycle focuses on the future suffering of the wicked at the final judgment.

- According to Revelation 14:12–13, what is the application for Christians after hearing the warnings of judgment issued to nonbelievers?

  After the first three angels appear with their warnings against the unbelieving world, Revelation 14:12–13 conveys words of application to believers. In light of the terrible judgment to come, God's people are called to persevere. Those who persevere are assured that when they die, they will rest from their labors, and the testimony of their lives will serve as a confirmation of their union with Christ.

After the Video

- According to Dr. Godfrey, what does the number 666 actually mean? How does this meaning offer encouragement to Christians?

  Rather than attempt to identify a historical figure through gematria or other methods, Dr. Godfrey takes a simpler approach. As Revelation 12–13 has shown, Satan unsuccessfully attempts to imitate God. The number of the beast is another instance of the devil's counterfeiting tendency. While the number of God's perfection is seven, the devil cannot attain it. Therefore, instead of attaining 777, the closest that Satan can achieve is 666. Christians can thus be encouraged that although the beast will cause havoc for God's people, he will ultimately never succeed in his purposes.

- What picture of the church emerges from Revelation's fourth literary cycle? What kind of progression is described?

  In the first vision of Revelation's fourth cycle, the church appears as a pregnant woman who is in agony and afflicted by suffering. In the seventh vision, the church appears in a state of triumph and rejoicing. The progression described in this cycle offers God's people hope that, despite their struggles, the church will emerge from its afflictions with success and blessing.

- What does Babylon represent? How is Babylon introduced in the book of Revelation? Why is this significant?

  Dr. Godfrey argues that Babylon appears in Revelation as a representation of political power. The first mention of Babylon in Revelation appears in 14:8. Although Babylon features prominently in later chapters of Revelation, this introduction in chapter 14 is significant because the first thing readers learn about this great harlot is that she has fallen; despite her former wealth and influence, her power has been utterly broken.

REVIEW QUIZ

Lesson 15

1. **A.**
   The term gematria *refers to alphanumeric systems that assign numerical values to certain letters in order to calculate numbers that pertain to certain words or names. Gematria is commonly appealed to as a way of deciphering the identity of the beast.*

2. **D.**
   Revelation's fourth cycle describes the continuous efforts of the devil to subdue or destroy the church. However, the seventh vision of this cycle portrays the church's final triumph after enduring persecution and exile.

3. **A.**
   The description of the saints as "blameless" in Revelation 14:5 does not suggest that they are morally perfect or sinless but rather suggests that they are faithful to God's covenant; that is, they have remained faithful to the Lord in the face of persecution and temptation.

4. **B.**
   Revelation's fifth cycle is shaped by seven angelic appearances, but one of these is a second appearance by a particular angel. Therefore, only six angels appear in this cycle.

5. **A.**
   Revelation 14:6–7 describes the opportunity for repentance that is extended to the inhabitants of the earth. Judgment comes after they are given the chance to turn from their wickedness, fear God, and worship Him.

6. **C.**
   One of the main regional superpowers of the ancient Near East, Babylon was known primarily for its great military power.

16

The Vindication of the Saints

INTRODUCTION

God will leave nothing undone. As John continues to relate his heavenly vision, the unfolding story of Revelation is one of completion. When the harvest of God's elect is ready to be gathered, Jesus will welcome every saint into His fold; when the hour of judgment arrives, God will answer the martyrs' unresolved cry for justice; when the heavenly host observe God's treatment of the righteous and the wicked, they will erupt with praise and adoration for His holiness, justice, and truth. Christians in all ages can take heart that God is at work and will not fail to accomplish His purposes.

LEARNING GOALS

When you have finished this lesson, you should be able to:

- Describe the structure and message of Revelation's fifth and sixth literary cycles
- Explain a biblical view of God's judgment and mercy

KEY IDEAS

- The time is coming when the harvest will be complete and God will gather His people.
- God will answer the cries of His saints for justice and vindication.
- God is glorified both when He extends mercy to the repentant and when He carries out justice against the unrepentant.

REFLECTION & DISCUSSION QUESTIONS

Before the Video

What Do You Think?

Take a moment to answer the following questions. They will prepare you for the lecture.

- Is the concept of judgment largely accepted or rejected in our culture? Why is that the case?

- Interact with the statement "True Christianity is being able to read statistics with sympathy." What is true in this statement? What is this statement missing?

Scripture Reading

And I saw what appeared to be a sea of glass mingled with fire—and also those who had conquered the beast and its image and the number of its name, standing beside the sea of glass with harps of God in their hands. And they sing the song of Moses, the servant of God, and the song of the Lamb, saying, "Great and amazing are your deeds, O Lord God the Almighty! Just and true are your ways, O King of the nations! Who will not fear, O Lord, and glorify your name? For you alone are holy. All nations will come and worship you, for your righteous acts have been revealed."

—Revelation 15:2–4

- What actions and attributes of God do these verses celebrate? What future events do they anticipate?

During the Video

Answer the following questions while you watch the video. They will guide you through the lecture.

The Harvest of the Earth *0:00–5:06*

- Which two figures bear a sickle in Revelation 14:14–19? What two distinct harvests are represented in these verses?

- How does Dr. Godfrey describe the overarching purpose of Revelation's fifth cycle?

The Bowls of God's Wrath *5:06–14:54*

- What is the literary relationship between Revelation's second and sixth cycles?

- What is the relationship between the instructions given to the angels in Revelation 16:1 and the Great Commission of Matthew 28:18–20?

Judgment and Justice *14:54–23:49*

- Is the intense judgment of the Lord poured out in Revelation 16 just or unjust? Explain.

- According to Revelation 16:9, how do the wicked respond to judgment? What Old Testament figure(s) responded to judgment in a similar way?

After the Video

Answer the following questions after you have finished the lecture. They will help you identify and summarize the major points.

- Read Mark 4:26–29. What is the connection between these verses and Revelation 14:14–16? What picture of Jesus do these two passages present?

  If you are in a group, have the members discuss the importance of sharing the good news of Jesus Christ. What role are Christians called to play in the harvest of God's people?

- How do the golden bowls from cycle 2 reappear in cycle 6?

  If you are in a group, have the members discuss what this correspondence between cycles 2 and 6 teaches about prayer. What is a prayer that you are still waiting for God to answer?

- According to Dr. Godfrey, what happens when Christians start down the path of thinking that we are more loving than God is? What is the likely reason behind our squeamishness about God's judgment?

  If you are in a group, have the members discuss ways that you have seen this kind of discomfort with divine judgment among Christians. Do you agree with Dr. Godfrey's analysis? Why or why not?

PRAYER

Commit what you have learned from God's Word in this lesson to prayer.

- Praise God for giving mercy to those who repent and justice to those who do not.
- Confess your own tendency to minimize the severity of human sin.
- Thank God for giving you mercy that you do not deserve instead of the justice that you do deserve.

- Ask God to give you boldness and compassion to proclaim the good news to people you know who do not believe in Jesus.

REVIEW QUIZ

Use these multiple-choice questions to measure what you learned from this lesson.

1. Which of the following Old Testament judgment scenes prefigures Revelation 14:20?
   a. The death of all firstborn
   b. The drowning of Pharaoh's army in the Red Sea
   c. The Nile's turning to blood
   d. The plague of locusts

2. Which of the following best describes the central message of Revelation's fifth literary cycle?
   a. That God will answer the prayers of the saints
   b. That judgment will fall on the wicked
   c. That the beast will be utterly destroyed
   d. That the righteous will be saved

3. Which of the following best describes the relationship between the Old and New Testaments in the book of Revelation?
   a. Describing two separate but complementary plans of salvation
   b. Focusing on two different audiences
   c. Vacillating between God's wrath and God's love
   d. Woven together into one message of redemption

4. The songs featured in the book of Revelation bear a resemblance to which of the following?
   a. Battle hymns
   b. Laments
   c. Messianic prophecies
   d. Psalms

5. What kind of additional "mark" will the people who received the mark of the beast also receive?
   a. Baptism
   b. Burning coal on their lips
   c. Painful sores
   d. Remorse over their sins

6. The "altar" that speaks in Revelation 16:7 refers to whom?
   a. Beasts
   b. Four living creatures
   c. Souls of the martyrs
   d. Twenty-four elders

Answer Key—The Vindication of the Saints

REFLECTION & DISCUSSION QUESTIONS

Before the Video

What Do You Think?

These are personal questions. The answers should be based on your own knowledge and experience.

Scripture Reading

- What actions and attributes of God do these verses celebrate? What future events do they anticipate?

  These verses represent the heavenly celebration of God's people who have conquered the beast and withstood his war against the saints. Their victory song praises God for His holiness, justice, and truth. It also celebrates His deeds of redemption and His righteous acts. References to Moses and the Lamb point to His act of rescuing His people from slavery in Egypt and from bondage to sin. In light of God's character and deeds, this song anticipates that all will fear the Lord and that all nations will come to worship Him.

During the Video

The Harvest of the Earth

- Which two figures bear a sickle in Revelation 14:14–19? What two distinct harvests are represented in these verses?

  One of the sickles in this passage is found in the hand of Jesus. In Revelation 14:15–16, this sickle is used to gather up all of God's people for the harvest. A second sickle appears in the hand of an angel in Revelation 14:17. This sickle is used to gather up the wicked at the final judgment so that they can be cast into the great winepress of the wrath of God.

- How does Dr. Godfrey describe the overarching purpose of Revelation's fifth cycle?

  Dr. Godfrey observed that the point of the fifth cycle is to remind God's people that judgment will fall on the wicked. They were called to repent. They have heard about God's deliverance of the saints. Rather than repent of their idolatry and rejection of God, they persist in their ways, and terrible judgment will fall on them.

The Bowls of God's Wrath

- What is the literary relationship between Revelation's second and sixth cycles?

  Due to the chiastic arrangement of Revelation's seven literary cycles, the second cycle corresponds to the sixth cycle. A key feature of the second cycle is the prayers of the saints under the altar, who ask, "How long, O Lord, until we are vindicated?" The second cycle describes the prayers of the saints as incense rising up from golden bowls. In the sixth cycle, the bowls that were emptied in prayer are now filled with God's answer to those prayers. As the wicked receive God's judgment in response to those prayers, the martyred saints are at last vindicated.

- What is the relationship between the instructions given to the angels in Revelation 16:1 and the Great Commission of Matthew 28:18–20?

  The instructions given to the angels in Revelation 16:1 represent the antithesis of the Great Commission in Matthew 28:18–20. The Great Commission is to go and tell about the salvation that God brings to all who respond. In contrast, the angels are told to go and take judgment to those who would not listen and would not respond.

Judgment and Justice

- Is the intense judgment of the Lord poured out in Revelation 16 just or unjust? Explain.

  Although the severity of the judgment described in Revelation 16 may seem unjustly harsh to modern readers, this passage reveals that this divine retribution is proportionate to the wrongdoing that had been committed. In fact, the justice of God's actions is affirmed by the angels and martyrs in heaven in verses 5–7.

- According to Revelation 16:9, how do the wicked respond to judgment? What Old Testament figure(s) responded to judgment in a similar way?

  Revelation 16:9 reports that, rather than repenting and giving glory to God, those who are afflicted by this plague curse God. This response to judgment is similar to the response of Job's wife, who urged Job to curse God and die. It is also a reminder of Pharaoh, who responded to God's displays of power with a hardened heart.

After the Video

- Read Mark 4:26–29. What is the connection between these verses and Revelation 14:14–16? What picture of Jesus do these two passages present?

  In Mark 4:26–29, Jesus describes the kingdom of heaven in terms of crops that are ripening in preparation for the harvest. Revelation 14 describes the moment when the crops have fully matured and are ready to be harvested. The picture of Jesus that we see in these passages is one of Jesus' reaping the great harvest of His people.

- How do the golden bowls from cycle 2 reappear in cycle 6?

  In Revelation's second cycle, the prayers of the saints are represented as incense in golden bowls. In cycle 6, the angels emerge from the temple bearing golden bowls, out of which the wrath of God is poured on the nations. Having been emptied of the prayers of the saints for vindication, these bowls are now filled with God's answer to those prayers.

- According to Dr. Godfrey, what happens when Christians start down the path of thinking that we are more loving than God is? What is the likely reason behind our squeamishness about God's judgment?

  Dr. Godfrey warns that if Christians start down the path of thinking that we are more loving than God is, we will end up with a God who has no judgment at all. We will end up supposing that we are wiser than God, attempt to "correct" God's Word, and find ourselves in the same state of theological confusion that has engulfed so much of the modern church. Dr. Godfrey surmises that our squeamishness about divine judgment may come in part from our own reluctance to recognize the gravity of our own sin. Our sinful nature seeks to suppress the truth that, apart from God's grace, we deserve the same judgment that the wicked in Revelation receive.

REVIEW QUIZ

Lesson 16

1. **C.**
   The description in Revelation 14:20 of the river of blood flowing from the winepress of the wrath of God is evocative of the scene in Exodus 7:20–24 when God instructed Moses to turn the Nile River into blood.

2. **B.**
   Dr. Godfrey pointed out that the purpose of Revelation's fifth literary cycle is to remind God's people that judgment will fall on the wicked. They were called to repent but instead turned their back and persisted in their sins. As a result of rejecting God, severe judgment will fall on them.

3. **D.**
   The book of Revelation presents the Old and New Testaments as woven together, communicating the same message of God and of His act of redeeming a people for Himself.

4. **D.**
   Dr. Godfrey made the observation that all the songs in the book of Revelation, particularly the song recorded in Revelation 15:3–4, bear a close resemblance to various compositions from the book of Psalms.

5. **C.**

   Revelation 16:2 records the plague of painful sores that will afflict those who bear the mark of the beast. Dr. Godfrey pointed out the irony that those who have previously received the beast's mark will now be "marked" by God as an act of judgment.

6. **C.**

   The reference to the "altar" speaking in Revelation 16:7 is actually a reference to the souls of the martyrs' crying out from beneath the altar for vindication in Revelation 6:9–11. Ten chapters later, these martyrs cry out with satisfaction that God has vindicated them by judging the wicked.

17

Plagues, Armageddon, & the Wrath of God

INTRODUCTION

As we approach the final cycle of Revelation, John recapitulates major themes of this book with increasing clarity and intensity. In this lesson, which completes the sixth cycle, we find that the wicked persist in their wickedness, the righteous are called to be always alert and ready, and all heavenly and earthly powers will one day bow before the triumphant Lamb.

LEARNING GOALS

When you have finished this lesson, you should be able to:

- Describe the conclusion and themes of Revelation's sixth literary cycle
- Summarize what will take place at Armageddon
- Identify common features between the ten plagues of Egypt and the seven plagues of Revelation 16

KEY IDEAS

- Followers of the beast will persist in their opposition to God regardless of the cost.
- God will utterly vanquish every earthly and supernatural power that rises up against Him.
- Jesus urges His followers to remain alert and prepared for Him to return at any moment.

REFLECTION & DISCUSSION QUESTIONS

Before the Video

What Do You Think?

Take a moment to answer the following questions. They will prepare you for the lecture.

- What comes to mind when you hear the word *Armageddon*?

- If Jesus returned to earth today, would you feel prepared? Why or why not?

Scripture Reading

For not from the east or from the west and not from the wilderness comes lifting up, but it is God who executes judgment, putting down one and lifting up another. For in the hand of the Lord *there is a cup with foaming wine, well mixed, and he pours out from it, and all the wicked of the earth shall drain it down to the dregs. But I will declare it forever; I will sing praises to the God of Jacob. All the horns of the wicked I will cut off, but the horns of the righteous shall be lifted up.*

—Psalm 75:6–10

- What imagery is used to describe God's kindness toward His people? What imagery is used in this passage to describe God's judgment on the wicked? How does this passage fit with themes that we've seen so far in Revelation?

During the Video

Answer the following questions while you watch the video. They will guide you through the lecture.

The Fifth and Sixth Bowls *0:00–13:16*

- At whom is the fifth plague of Revelation's sixth cycle directed? What is the result of this plague?

- How do the second and sixth cycles of Revelation offer a similar picture of the kings of the earth?

The Seventh Bowl *13:16–22:47*

- What are the two possible ways for sinners to bring their problem with sin to an end?

- What echoes of the ten plagues on Egypt appear in Revelation's sixth cycle?

After the Video

Answer the following questions after you have finished the lecture. They will help you identify and summarize the major points.

- Read 2 Kings 23:28–30. What was the outcome of the Battle of Megiddo? What is the final outcome of Armageddon in Revelation 16:12–16?

  If you are in a group, have the members identify and describe instances of human defiance against God. How do these instances typically end?

- According to Dr. Godfrey, what is the best way for Christians to prepare themselves for the battle of Armageddon?

  If you are in a group, have the members read Ephesians 6:10–18. Which part of the armor of God do you wear most naturally? Which part of this heavenly armor is the most challenging for you?

- Revelation 16:15 declares, "Blessed is the one who stays awake, keeping his garments on, that he may not go about naked and be seen exposed!" What does it mean for believers to stay awake and keep their garments on?

  If you are in a group, have the members discuss the following question: How should the expectation of Christ's return influence the way Christians approach day-to-day life?

PRAYER

Commit what you have learned from God's Word in this lesson to prayer.

- Praise God for His sovereign power over nature, human kingdoms, and demonic forces.
- Confess any areas of your life where your heart has been hardened toward God or others.
- Thank God for defending you from the schemes of the beast and his followers.
- Ask God to help you to remain spiritually alert and prepared for Christ's return.

REVIEW QUIZ

Use these multiple-choice questions to measure what you learned from this lesson.

1. The beast's followers will refuse to repent until the plague of darkness changes their minds.
   a. True
   b. False

2. The drying up of which major river permits the kings from the east to assemble in battle against the Lord in Revelation 16:12?
   a. Euphrates
   b. Jordan
   c. Nile
   d. Tigris

3. Which Near Eastern leader died in the ancient Battle of Megiddo?
   a. Hezekiah
   b. Josiah
   c. Neco
   d. Sennacherib

4. Which of the following best describes the meaning of "stays awake" in Revelation 16:15?
   a. Being ready for Jesus to return at any time
   b. Figuring out the true identity of the antichrist
   c. Maintaining a state of productive busyness
   d. Minimizing physical rest

5. Which of the following plagues appears in Revelation's sixth cycle but not in the ten plagues on Egypt?
   a. Boils or sores on the skin
   b. Darkness covering the land
   c. Tremendous earthquake
   d. Water turning into blood

6. Which literary cycle is the longest in the book of Revelation?
   a. Cycle 1
   b. Cycle 5
   c. Cycle 6
   d. Cycle 7

Answer Key—
Plagues, Armageddon, & the Wrath of God

REFLECTION & DISCUSSION QUESTIONS

Before the Video

What Do You Think?

These are personal questions. The answers should be based on your own knowledge and experience.

Scripture Reading

- What imagery is used to describe God's kindness toward His people? What imagery is used in this passage to describe God's judgment on the wicked? How does this passage fit with themes that we've seen so far in Revelation?

  Psalm 75 powerfully describes God's sovereignty over the righteous and the wicked. Three times God's care for the righteous is presented as an act of "lifting up," which is echoed in Revelation's description of God's delivering His people from hardship and vindicating their sufferings. This psalm also presents vivid imagery associated with judgment on the wicked. God is described as putting down the wicked, cutting off their horns (evocative of the horns on the beasts of Rev. 13), and causing them to drink from the cup of His wrath (evocative of the bowls of God's wrath in Rev. 16), draining it to the dregs.

During the Video

The Fifth and Sixth Bowls

- At whom is the fifth plague of Revelation's sixth cycle directed? What is the result of this plague?

  The fifth plague of this cycle, the plague of darkness, specifically targets the throne of the beast and his kingdom. Although this plague reveals the hopelessness of the beast's cause, his followers do not repent and submit to God. Rather, they gnaw their tongues in anguish and curse the name of God.

- How do the second and sixth cycles of Revelation offer a similar picture of the kings of the earth?

  In the second cycle, Revelation 6:15 depicts kings, generals, and "great ones" of the earth hiding themselves in caves in a futile effort to escape God's judgment. Revelation 16:12 shows kings and generals out in the open, assembling for a futile battle against God. Both of these passages reveal the defiance of earthly leaders against the God of heaven, and both of these passages indicate that they are powerless to escape His justice.

The Seventh Bowl

- What are the two possible ways for sinners to bring their problem with sin to an end?

  The angel's proclamation "It is done!" in Revelation 16:17 represents a parallel with the final words of Jesus on the cross. These parallel pronouncements highlight the two ways that sinners can have their problem with sin brought to an end. One way is for sinners to have Jesus pay for their sins on the cross. The alternative is for sinners to pay for their sins themselves at the last judgment. Either way, human sin must be dealt with by a Holy God.

- What echoes of the ten plagues on Egypt appear in Revelation's sixth cycle?

  The seven plagues in the sixth cycle of Revelation repeat many of the same plagues that appear in Exodus 6–12. Among them are outbreaks of painful sores, water turning to blood, darkness that covers the land, and large hailstones. Another similarity between the plagues in Exodus and the plagues in Revelation is the fact that those who are afflicted, like Pharaoh of Egypt, harden their hearts against God and do not repent.

After the Video

- Read 2 Kings 23:28–30. What was the outcome of the Battle of Megiddo? What is the final outcome of Armageddon in Revelation 16:12–16?

  The outcome of the Battle of Megiddo was the death of King Josiah of Judah in a conflict between the superpowers of Egypt and Assyria. The final outcome of Armageddon, described in Revelation 16, is that the superpowers of the earth will come together against God and will all come to nothing. Neither human might nor the satanic power of the beast can triumph over the triune God.

- According to Dr. Godfrey, what is the best way for Christians to prepare themselves for the battle of Armageddon?

  Dr. Godfrey contended that Christians should not prepare for a literal battle or attempt to fight Satan with instruments of earthly warfare. Rather, the best way to prepare for the moment of Armageddon is to believe in Christ and live as His faithful follower.

- Revelation 16:15 declares, "Blessed is the one who stays awake, keeping his garments on, that he may not go about naked and be seen exposed!" What does it mean for believers to stay awake and keep their garments on?

  Rather than a warning against physical sleep or nakedness, this verse is an exhortation for believers to remain spiritually prepared for Christ's return. Rather than being spiritually unclothed, we are to adorn ourselves in the robes of righteousness received by faith in Christ. Instead of succumbing to spiritual sloth, we should remain spiritually alert and active, faithful in service to our risen and returning King.

REVIEW QUIZ

Lesson 17

1. **B.**
   Even the plague of darkness in Revelation 16:10 will not bring the beast's followers to repentance. Instead, they will curse God and persist in their sins.

2. **A.**
   Revelation 16:12 reports that the drying up of the Euphrates prepares the way for the kings from the east to assemble against the Lord. Dr. Godfrey pointed out that this description is likely intended to be viewed symbolically.

3. **B.**
   As a result of his alliance with the king of Assyria, King Josiah of Judah became embroiled in conflict with Pharaoh Neco of Egypt and was struck down by the Egyptians in the Battle of Megiddo, as recorded in 2 Kings 23:28–30.

4. **A.**
   Rather than interpreting the exhortation to stay awake in Revelation 16:15 as a warning against physical rest, we should see this statement as a reminder to live faithfully for Christ and be ready for Him to return at any time.

5. **C.**
   Many of the plagues recorded in Revelation 16—such as painful boils, large hailstones, darkness, and water turning into blood—also took place in Egypt during the time of Moses. However, the terrible earthquake mentioned in Revelation 16:18 does not have a precedent in the Egyptian plagues.

6. **D.**
   Dr. Godfrey observed that Revelation's seventh cycle, which runs from chapter 17 into the first verses of chapter 22, is by far the longest cycle in the book of Revelation. We will begin to explore the seventh cycle in lesson 18.

18

The Splendor & Fall of Babylon the Great

INTRODUCTION

Revelation's seventh cycle begins with a vivid and detailed description of Babylon. Appearing as a prostitute who has seduced many nations and peoples, Babylon exudes arrogance, indulgence, and self-glorification. However exalted and unconquerable she may appear, the angels announce that her doom is certain. In this lesson, Dr. Godfrey will examine John's account of Babylon the great, noting the warning, hope, and encouragement that this narrative offers to God's people.

LEARNING GOALS

When you have finished this lesson, you should be able to:

- Describe the structure and message of Revelation's seventh literary cycle
- Identify key characteristics of Babylon the prostitute
- Describe Babylon's role in history and the outcome that awaits Babylon in the future

KEY IDEAS

- Throughout history, the corrupt political power of Babylon is allied with the corrupt religious power of the beast.
- Many manifestations of Babylon surface throughout history, each opposing God and oppressing God's people.
- Like the beast, Babylon will receive God's swift and decisive judgment.

REFLECTION & DISCUSSION QUESTIONS

Before the Video

What Do You Think?

Take a moment to answer the following questions. They will prepare you for the lecture.

- In what ways can political and religious power become aligned? What dangers might this kind of alliance present?

- What are practical ways that Christians can live in the world but not of the world?

Scripture Reading

Then I heard another voice from heaven saying, "Come out of her, my people, lest you take part in her sins, lest you share in her plagues; for her sins are heaped high as heaven, and God has remembered her iniquities. Pay her back as she herself has paid back others, and repay her double for her deeds; mix a double portion for her in the cup she mixed. As she glorified herself and lived in luxury, so give her a like measure of torment and mourning, since in her heart she says, 'I sit as a queen, I am no widow, and mourning I shall never see.' For this reason her plagues will come in a single day, death and mourning and famine, and she will be burned up with fire; for mighty is the Lord God who has judged her."

—Revelation 18:4–8

- How do these verses describe Babylon's pride? How do these verses describe the judgment that will fall on her?

During the Video

Answer the following questions while you watch the video. They will guide you through the lecture.

The Splendor of Babylon *0:00–18:19*

- Describe the chiastic structure of Revelation's seventh cycle.

- Is the scarlet beast of Revelation 17:3 one of the beasts seen before or a different beast? Explain.

- What is the relationship between Rome and Babylon? What does it mean that there will be many manifestations of Babylon?

The Fall of Babylon *18:19–24:04*

- How does Dr. Godfrey summarize the judgment that falls swiftly on Babylon?

- How does the warning of Babylon's fall offer hope to the people of God?

After the Video

Answer the following questions after you have finished the lecture. They will help you identify and summarize the major points.

- Read Revelation 1:8 and 17:8. How do these verses highlight the beast's inability to compete with God?

  If you are in a group, have the members discuss Satan's fruitless efforts to counterfeit God's character and deeds. In what way is "aping"—Dr. Godfrey's preferred term for this activity—an appropriate description of Satan's behavior?

- What is the point of the ten kings mentioned in Revelation 17:12–14?

  If you are in a group, have the members discuss the ever-present power of Babylon throughout human history. In addition to ancient Rome, what are some other possible manifestations of Babylon in the past? Where might we see the traits of Babylon—pride, materialism, luxury—at work in our own culture?

- Read Revelation 18:4. How is the call for God's people to come out from Babylon best understood?

  If you are in a group, have the members discuss different approaches that Christians sometimes take when it comes to separating ourselves from the world. What do you find helpful in these approaches? What do you find unhelpful in them?

PRAYER

Commit what you have learned from God's Word in this lesson to prayer.

- Praise God for His divine justice that will not allow wickedness to go unpunished.

- Confess areas of your life where you are tempted by the pride, indulgence, and luxury that Babylon represents.
- Thank God that He will bring Babylon's persecution of His people to an end.
- Ask God to help you flee from the temptations of Babylon and live as a faithful witness of a better kingdom.

REVIEW QUIZ

Use these multiple-choice questions to measure what you learned from this lesson.

1. What forms the center of the chiastic structure of Revelation's seventh cycle?
   a. Celebration of the Lamb's victory
   b. Judgment on the beast and the dragon
   c. Lament for fallen Babylon
   d. Praise to God for what He has done
2. What detail at the beginning of Revelation 17 ties the sixth and seventh cycles together?
   a. Angel with a bowl
   b. Earthquake
   c. Horns on the beast
   d. Wilderness
3. What kind of corrupt power does Babylon primarily represent?
   a. Cultural influence
   b. Military might
   c. Political power
   d. Religious persuasion
4. With what has the woman Babylon become drunk?
   a. Blood of the martyrs
   b. Political corruption
   c. Pride
   d. Sexual immorality
5. Throughout the book of Revelation, sequence consistently communicates chronology.
   a. True
   b. False
6. Over what duration of time will Babylon's judgment take place?
   a. 1 day
   b. 7 days
   c. 40 days
   d. 7 years

Answer Key—The Splendor & Fall of Babylon the Great

REFLECTION & DISCUSSION QUESTIONS

Before the Video

What Do You Think?

These are personal questions. The answers should be based on your own knowledge and experience.

Scripture Reading

- How do these verses describe Babylon's pride? How do these verses describe the judgment that will fall on her?

  These verses paint a vivid picture of Babylon's lavish lifestyle and immense pride. She is described as glorifying herself and living in luxury. She proclaims herself to be a queen and denies that she will ever experience mourning. These verses describe not only the extent of Babylon's wickedness and hubris but also her impending doom. This passage affirms that God has not forgotten her iniquities and will pay her back double for her wickedness. Within a single day, she will fall victim to plagues, death, mourning, famine, and a consuming fire.

During the Video

The Splendor of Babylon

- Describe the chiastic structure of Revelation's seventh cycle.

  Like many of the other literary cycles in Revelation, the seventh and final cycle is arranged chiastically. The first section of this cycle, describing the harlot Babylon, is paired with the seventh section, which describes the bride of Christ. The second section, describing the judgment on Babylon, is paired with the sixth section, describing the judgment on the beast and the dragon. The third section, a lament for Babylon, contrasts with the fifth section, a celebration of the Lamb's victory. The fourth section, the very heart of the seventh cycle, is a song of praise to God for all that He has done.

- Is the scarlet beast of Revelation 17:3 one of the beasts seen before or a different beast? Explain.

  Strictly speaking, Revelation 17:3 contains the first appearance of a scarlet beast. However, Dr. Godfrey argues that John is not introducing a separate, third beast into the narrative. Rather, this beast represents a conflation of the fiery dragon and the beast from the sea. Once the symbols of Revelation are understood, they can be rearranged in certain ways throughout the book while keeping a similar meaning. John is describing the same characters in a different way in order to illustrate the alliance between the corrupt political power of Babylon and the corrupt religious power of the beast.

- What is the relationship between Rome and Babylon? What does it mean that there will be many manifestations of Babylon?

  The reference in Revelation 17:9 to "seven mountains on which the woman is seated" is probably an allusion to the city of Rome, which was built on seven hills. However, while Rome fits this imagery, it does not completely fulfill the role of Babylon. When Dr. Godfrey points out that there will be many manifestations of Babylon, he is noting that Babylon is a symbolic figure that is present throughout human history. While ancient Rome surely was the dominant expression of Babylon in the first century, other expressions of Babylon have come and gone in the centuries that followed. The discussion of the ten kings in Revelation 17:12–14 also fits this paradigm. The kings are best understood not as an alliance of powerful contemporaries but as a sequence of like-minded manifestations of Babylon throughout history.

The Fall of Babylon

- How does Dr. Godfrey summarize the judgment that falls swiftly on Babylon?

  Dr. Godfrey summarized Babylon's impending doom as a judgment of utter desolation. She who was so proud, so confident, so sure that she would never be cast down, so caught up in luxurious living, shall be utterly desolate, utterly abandoned, and utterly destroyed.

- How does the warning of Babylon's fall offer hope to the people of God?

  Revelation 18:1–8 issues a clear warning of Babylon's inevitable fall. These verses declare that all the arrogance, apparent power, and apparent success of Babylon will come crashing down. Her judgment is sure, and her end is coming. This warning offers hope to God's people that, however greatly they may be persecuted in every age, their persecution will come to an end, and their persecutors will face justice.

After the Video

- Read Revelation 1:8 and 17:8. How do these verses highlight the beast's inability to compete with God?

  In contrast with the description of God as the One who was, and is, and is to come, the beast is described as one who was, and is not, and will go to destruction. This comparison reveals how pathetic the beast's power is in light of the matchless power of God.

- What is the point of the ten kings mentioned in Revelation 17:12–14?

  Revelation 17:12–14 mentions ten kings in association with Babylon and the beast. These kings have not yet received their power but will be allowed to rule for one hour with the beast. They align themselves with the beast and wage war against the Lamb. The point of the reference to ten kings is not that ten specific human rulers will appear at the end times to help the beast but that throughout human history a long line of earthly powers will rise, rule for a short time, and fade. Although there will be many manifestations of Babylon, they will all represent the same kind of corrupt political power in league with corrupt religious practice.

- Read Revelation 18:4. How is the call for God's people to come out from Babylon best understood?

  This call in Revelation 18:4 is not a call to physical separation or withdrawal from society. Rather, it is a call for Christians to separate themselves from sin, to separate themselves from the values and lifestyle of Babylon, and to separate themselves from her self-centeredness and indulgence. It is a call to be in the world but not of the world, to bear faithful witness to Christ in the midst of a fallen culture.

REVIEW QUIZ

Lesson 18

1. **D.**
   The outer layer of the chiastic structure of this cycle contrasts the harlot Babylon in the first section with the bride of Christ in the seventh section. The second and sixth sections describe God's judgment on Babylon and then on the beast and the dragon. The inner ring of the chiasm contrasts the third section's lament for Babylon with the fifth section's celebration of the Lamb's victory. The fourth section, the heart of the seventh cycle, is a song of praise to God for all that He has done.

2. **A.**
   Revelation 17 opens with one of the seven angels' bearing the seven bowls of wrath. This angel, which appeared in the previous cycle, carries John to the wilderness, where he sees Babylon the prostitute in the first scene of the seventh cycle.

3. **C.**
   Babylon the prostitute is a vivid representation of corrupt political power. Rather than representing a specific political state or regime, she represents the ever-present political corruption that surfaces again and again throughout human history.

4. **A.**
   Revelation 17:6 reports that John "saw the woman, drunk with the blood of the saints, the blood of the martyrs of Jesus." This description reveals that Babylon is guilty not just of political corruption in general but of persecuting and killing the people of God.

5. **B.**
   Dr. Godfrey pointed out that when studying Revelation, it is important to remember that the sequence in which details are presented does not necessarily communicate the chronological order in which things happen. Rather, John uses sequence to elaborate on the basic point being made. In other words, Revelation often presents content by topic or theme rather than in the order that events take place.

6. **A.**
   According to Revelation 18:8, Babylon's judgment will be swift and terrible, taking place in a single day.

19

The Wicked Lament & the Saints Rejoice

INTRODUCTION

After describing the hubris and fall of the great prostitute Babylon, John describes the dismayed reaction of the global powers who benefited from her indulgent reign. In contrast to the bitter sorrow of the wicked at Babylon's demise, John also presents the chorus of praise that erupts from the poor and lowly when this oppressive mistress meets her end. He then points his readers forward to the glorious scene surrounding the marriage supper of the Lamb, when the church will emerge as a dazzling bride ready to take her place at Jesus' side.

LEARNING GOALS

When you have finished this lesson, you should be able to:

- Contrast the two prominent women in Revelation's seventh cycle: the prostitute Babylon and the bride of Christ
- Describe the loss that the wicked feel when Babylon is destroyed
- Describe the praise and vindication of the righteous when evil is dealt with

KEY IDEAS

- The account of Babylon's destruction invites all people to slow down and consider what they are living for.
- While Babylon offers enticement to the rich and powerful, the bride of Christ offers hope and belonging to the poor and powerless.
- The righteous can rejoice at the fall of Babylon, knowing that the glorious union between Jesus and His bride is at hand.

REFLECTION & DISCUSSION QUESTIONS

Before the Video

What Do You Think?

Take a moment to answer the following questions. They will prepare you for the lecture.

- Have you experienced the loss of something important to you? What was this experience like?

- What are the benefits of material prosperity? What are the dangers?

Scripture Reading

Then a mighty angel took up a stone like a great millstone and threw it into the sea, saying, "So will Babylon the great city be thrown down with violence, and will be found no more; and the sound of harpists and musicians, of flute players and trumpeters, will be heard in you no more, and a craftsman of any craft will be found in you no more, and the sound of the mill will be heard in you no more, and the light of a lamp will shine in you no more, and the voice of bridegroom and bride will be heard in you no more, for your merchants were the great ones of the earth, and all nations were deceived by your sorcery. And in her was found the blood of prophets and of saints, and of all who have been slain on earth."

—Revelation 18:21–24

- What reasons are given in this passage for Babylon's destruction? What powerful visual is used to describe the nature of her overthrow?

During the Video

Answer the following questions while you watch the video. They will guide you through the lecture.

The Lament for Fallen Babylon *0:00–11:54*

- What unique feature of Revelation 18:9–19 does Dr. Godfrey point out? What literary effect does this create on the pacing of the book as a whole?

- What three groups of people give voice to a lament? What are the common features of their laments?

Praise for the Triumphant God *11:54–23:49*

- What are the two topics of praise in Revelation 18:20–19:10?

- What difference does Dr. Godfrey note between the people who lament the fall of Babylon and the people who are commended as God's servants?

After the Video

Answer the following questions after you have finished the lecture. They will help you identify and summarize the major points.

- Is the lament for Babylon meant to be an attack on commerce and prosperity? Explain.

  If you are in a group, have the members read Matthew 19:21–24 and 1 Timothy 6:6–10. How is the spiritual danger of wealth presented in these verses? What warning should Christians in affluent societies take to heart from these passages?

- What does John attempt to do when he is overcome by the majesty of heavenly worship? What does the angel's response imply for the practice of Christian worship?

  If you are in a group, have the members discuss aspects of Christian worship that tend to take the focus off Christ. What can churches do to maintain purity of worship?

- Dr. Godfrey concluded this lesson with a discussion of the interplay between the Bible and human tradition at the time of the Reformation. What do you think is the right relationship between the Bible and tradition?

  If you are in a group, have the members discuss their experiences with various elements of human religious tradition (books, creeds, catechisms, hymns, church history, holidays, liturgical practices, etc.). What human traditions have been helpful to your spiritual growth? What human traditions have caused confusion or harm to your spiritual growth?

PRAYER

Commit what you have learned from God's Word in this lesson to prayer.

- Praise God for demonstrating His holiness in judgment and in redemption.

- Confess ways that your focus drifts toward Babylon instead of Christ's bride.
- Thank God for offering you a kingdom that is greater than Babylon in every way.
- Ask God to give you a greater hunger and thirst for righteousness as you anticipate the marriage supper of the Lamb.

REVIEW QUIZ

Use these multiple-choice questions to measure what you learned from this lesson.

1. Which group of people does not express a lament for the fallen city of Babylon?
   a. Kings
   b. Martyrs
   c. Merchants
   d. Sailors

2. The lament for Babylon illustrates how deeply people are motivated by which of the following?
   a. A sense of purpose
   b. Economic self-interest
   c. Moral conviction
   d. Religious fervor

3. The list of Babylon's imports in Revelation 18:11–13 includes all *except* which of the following?
   a. Cloth
   b. Horses and chariots
   c. Idols
   d. Slaves

4. The lament for Babylon in Revelation 18 and the commendation of Christ's servants in Revelation 19 begin at opposite ends of the socioeconomic spectrum.
   a. True
   b. False

5. According to Revelation 19:8, what kind of clothing is the bride of Christ wearing?
   a. A coat of many colors
   b. Expensive clothes of purple and scarlet
   c. Priestly raiment with fine gemstones
   d. Pure, bright linen

6. Revelation 19:10 offers a powerful argument for the veneration of angels.
   a. True
   b. False

Answer Key—The Wicked Lament & the Saints Rejoice

REFLECTION & DISCUSSION QUESTIONS

Before the Video

What Do You Think?

These are personal questions. The answers should be based on your own knowledge and experience.

Scripture Reading

- What reasons are given in this passage for Babylon's destruction? What powerful visual is used to describe the nature of her overthrow?

  These verses present three reasons for Babylon's destruction. First is her preoccupation with power and wealth, as expressed by the statement that her "merchants were the great ones of the earth." Next is her use of sorcery and enchantment to lead people not to look to God but to fixate on this world and its meaning. Finally, Babylon was led by her worldliness to kill the prophets of God and His saints who had been slain on earth. The nature of her abrupt destruction is presented in terms of a large stone being hurled into the sea; she will be thrown down with great violence and will be found no more.

During the Video

The Lament for Fallen Babylon

- What unique feature of Revelation 18:9–19 does Dr. Godfrey point out? What literary effect does this create on the pacing of the book as a whole?

  This section of Revelation is unique because it is perhaps the only place where the wicked speak in their own words. The considerable amount of time given to the lament of the wicked serves as a sort of literary device to build tension in the final cycle and delay the resolution that readers anticipate in the final judgment. The effect on the reader is an act of slowing down rather than rushing to the end of the book.

- What three groups of people give voice to a lament? What are the common features of their laments?

  The laments for Babylon that appear in Revelation 18:9–19 are voiced by three groups of people. The first group consists of the kings of the earth, described as committing sexual immorality with her and living in luxury with her. The second group consists of the merchants of the earth, who had grown wealthy selling luxurious trade goods to her. The third group consists of shipmasters and sailors, who gained their livelihood from the trade that she had generated. Common features of these three laments include the sudden nature of Babylon's fall and their distress over the effects of this calamity on them and on their livelihood.

Praise for the Triumphant God

- What are the two topics of praise in Revelation 18:20–19:10?

  The section of praise that spans Revelation 18:20–19:10 is twofold. First comes praise in 18:20–19:5 for the vindication of God's people in the judgment of Babylon. Praise for the wedding feast of the Lamb follows in 19:6–10.

- What difference does Dr. Godfrey note between the people who lament the fall of Babylon and the people who are commended as God's servants?

  In keeping with his earlier point that earthly empires are often built on the disparity between the powerful few who dwell in luxury and the masses who live in poverty, Dr. Godfrey noted that the lament for Babylon begins with the kings and great ones of the earth. In contrast, the commendation of God's servants in Revelation 19:5 begins with those described as "small." In contrast to Babylon, God does not overlook the lowly and poor.

After the Video

- Is the lament for Babylon meant to be an attack on commerce and prosperity? Explain.

  This section of Revelation should not be understood as an attack on good living or on buying and selling. However, it is intended to cause readers to slow down and think about what they are living for. The luxurious lifestyle of Babylon, dependent on the wide array of trade goods described in 18:11–13, led to a mind-set of worldliness and materialism that is starkly at odds with the values of God's kingdom.

- What does John attempt to do when he is overcome by the majesty of heavenly worship? What does the angel's response imply for the practice of Christian worship?

  In Revelation 19:10, John is so overcome by the glory of this heavenly worship that he falls down to worship the angel who is speaking to him. The angel commands him to worship God instead, for he is simply a fellow servant of Jesus. This verse reminds Christians not to equate holy or heavenly things with God and to maintain a pure and unrivaled focus on Christ in worship.

- Dr. Godfrey concluded this lesson with a discussion of the interplay between the Bible and human tradition at the time of the Reformation. What do you think is the right relationship between the Bible and tradition?

  The answer to this question is personal but should take into consideration Dr. Godfrey's discussion of different views on this topic. Often those who champion the equal authority of Scripture and tradition argue that there is no conflict between the two; yet, much of the tradition argued for in actuality contradicts the Bible. On the other hand, those who argue for the sole authority of Scripture and completely jettison all human tradition end up cutting themselves off from the wisdom of the past. The approach most frequently taken in the Reformed tradition is to affirm the authority of Scripture alone as our highest authority while also affirming the value of some forms of human tradition as secondary authorities insofar as they reflect scriptural truth.

REVIEW QUIZ

Lesson 19

1. **B.**
   Revelation 18 records words of lamentation for fallen Babylon uttered by kings, merchants, and sailors who are devastated by the loss of the personal benefits they received from the immoral city. On the other hand, the followers of Christ who were martyred at the hands of Babylon express praise to God for their long-awaited vindication.

2. **B.**
   The primary motivation expressed in the laments for fallen Babylon is financial self-interest. The kings, merchants, and sailors express distress, not over the loss of life that took place in Babylon's fall, but over the loss of their own personal economic prosperity.

3. **C.**
   The list of Babylon's imports that appears in Revelation 18:11–13 includes expensive cloth, chariots and horses, slaves, and a wide array of other consumer goods. Although the city is known for its spiritual darkness, idols do not appear on the list of imports.

4. **A.**
   The lament of the wicked begins with the kings and great ones of the earth and then moves down the socioeconomic scale to merchants and finally to sailors. In contrast, the commendation of Christ's servants in Revelation 19:5 begins with the "small" and ends with the "great."

5. **D.**
   In contrast with the gaudy, expensive clothing of scarlet and purple worn by the prostitute, the bride of Christ is described wearing fine linen, bright and pure.

6. **B.**
   Although John is tempted to worship an angel in Revelation 19:10, the angel rebukes him and instructs him to worship God instead. This verse is a vivid reminder of Jesus' words in Luke 4:8: "You shall worship the Lord your God, and him only shall you serve."

20

The Victorious Rider & the Chained Dragon

INTRODUCTION

The final chapters of Revelation present God's victory in increasingly clear and decisive terms. In this lesson, we will first examine what Revelation teaches about Jesus' triumph over the beast. Finally, we will discuss the period of one thousand years described in Revelation 20. Because God is in complete control and has limited Satan's power, the church can faithfully and fearlessly carry out her mission to proclaim the gospel of Jesus Christ to the ends of the earth.

LEARNING GOALS

When you have finished this lesson, you should be able to:

- Summarize the Bible's teaching on Christ's victory over the beast in Revelation 19:11–21 and the thousand-year period when Satan is chained in Revelation 20:1–6
- Describe the major interpretive approaches to the millennium of Revelation 20

KEY IDEAS

- As powerful as the beast and his allies may seem to be, Christ's victory over them will be swift, decisive, and absolute.
- Satan's power has been limited so that the church can fruitfully carry out the Great Commission to the ends of the earth.
- The church's suffering will be brief, and the church's victory will be everlasting.

REFLECTION & DISCUSSION QUESTIONS

Before the Video

What Do You Think?

Take a moment to answer the following questions. They will prepare you for the lecture.

- How do you picture the final battle between God and Satan? What images or ideas come to mind?

- In what area(s) of life are you most eager to see Jesus win the final victory over sin and darkness?

Scripture Reading

Then I saw heaven opened, and behold, a white horse! The one sitting on it is called Faithful and True, and in righteousness he judges and makes war. His eyes are like a flame of fire, and on his head are many diadems, and he has a name written that no one knows but himself. He is clothed in a robe dipped in blood, and the name by which he is called is The Word of God. And the armies of heaven, arrayed in fine linen, white and pure, were following him on white horses. From his mouth comes a sharp sword with which to strike down the nations, and he will rule them with a rod of iron. He will tread the winepress of the fury of the wrath of God the Almighty. On his robe and on his thigh he has a name written, King of kings and Lord of lords.

—Revelation 19:11–16

- Compare this description of Jesus to the description that appears in Revelation 1:12–18. What do these two passages have in common? How does Revelation 19 expand on the picture of Jesus presented earlier in this book?

During the Video

Answer the following questions while you watch the video. They will guide you through the lecture.

The Victorious Rider *0:00–8:33*

- What is the great supper of God? What is it a sign and representation of?

- How is the theme of final judgment expanded and elaborated on in cycles 5, 6, and 7?

The Millennium *8:33–25:13*

- Why would the reference to one thousand years have come as a surprise to the original audience of Revelation?

- What two distinct angles on the dragon are presented in Revelation 12 and 20?

After the Video

Answer the following questions after you have finished the lecture. They will help you identify and summarize the major points.

- What three views of the millennium does Dr. Godfrey present? Briefly summarize each.

  If you are in a group, have the members discuss what they see as the strengths and difficulties of each of these millennial views.

- How does Revelation 20:1 describe the angel that binds the dragon? Why is this significant?

  If you are in a group, have the members describe their perceptions of Satan's power and influence. How has your understanding of Satan's power and his war against the church changed or increased during this study of Revelation?

- What is the practical result of the chaining of the dragon for the church's mission today?

  If you are in a group, have the members discuss their perception of Satan's confinement. In what ways are you aware of the limits on his power? In what ways do his power and influence still seem overwhelming to you?

PRAYER

Commit what you have learned from God's Word in this lesson to prayer.

- Praise God for completely subduing all His and your enemies.
- Confess areas of your life where you feel restless, hurried, or overwhelmed.
- Thank God for giving the church ample time to accomplish its mission.
- Ask God to grant you peace and clarity as you serve Him in the midst of a rushed and uncertain world.

REVIEW QUIZ

Use these multiple-choice questions to measure what you learned from this lesson.

1. The phrase "great supper of God" refers to which of the following?
   a. The Lord's Supper
   b. Fellowship of the church
   c. Wedding feast of the Lamb
   d. Birds feasting on a fallen army

2. Revelation 20 is best understood as an appendix or epilogue to the rest of the book.
   a. True
   b. False

3. Which millennial position has been most common in the history of the church?
   a. Amillennialism
   b. Dispensational premillennialism
   c. Historic premillennialism
   d. Postmillennialism

4. Which millennial position has become dominant among American Protestants since the late nineteenth century?
   a. Amillennialism
   b. Dispensational premillennialism
   c. Historic premillennialism
   d. Postmillennialism

5. According to Dr. Godfrey, which of the following ought to be the first question asked about the millennium when reading Revelation 20?
   a. How can there be a thousand years?
   b. Is the period of a thousand years literal or symbolic?
   c. What exactly is the thousand years?
   d. When will the thousand years take place?

6. Which Scottish missionary argued that since Christ was never in a hurry, there is no need for Christians to hurry about their work?
   a. David Livingstone
   b. Eric Liddell
   c. John Knox
   d. Mary Slessor

Answer Key—The Victorious Rider & the Chained Dragon

REFLECTION & DISCUSSION QUESTIONS

Before the Video

What Do You Think?

These are personal questions. The answers should be based on your own knowledge and experience.

Scripture Reading

- Compare this description of Jesus to the description that appears in Revelation 1:12–18. What do these two passages have in common? How does Revelation 19 expand on the picture of Jesus presented earlier in this book?

  These two passages offer complementary pictures of Jesus. Both present Him wearing a robe, arrayed in brilliant white, with eyes like blazing fire, and with a sharp sword coming out of His mouth. While the first vision presents Jesus standing in the heavenly temple in the midst of His churches, this later vision portrays Him leading the host of heaven and the redeemed humanity to battle against the forces of darkness. Revelation 19 displays Christ as a conqueror, riding on a horse, wearing blood on His robes, and carrying out God's just judgment against the wicked.

During the Video

The Victorious Rider

- What is the great supper of God? What is it a sign and representation of?

  The "great supper of God," mentioned in Revelation 19:17, refers to the utter defeat of God's enemies, whose slain bodies will be left on the battlefield as carrion for the birds. This grisly image is a sign and representation of Christ's complete victory and of the utter devastation and elimination of those who rebel against Him.

- How is the theme of final judgment expanded and elaborated on in cycles 5, 6, and 7?

  The motif of final judgment first appears in Revelation's fifth cycle and reappears in greater detail in both of the following cycles. The fifth cycle presents the final judgment falling on Babylon and then on all humankind. In the sixth cycle, John's description of the final judgment expands to include Babylon, the beasts, the dragon, and then all humankind. Finally, the seventh cycle presents the final judgment in even greater detail, to include more vivid and lengthy portrayals of the judgments on Babylon, the beasts, the dragon, and all humankind, spanning Revelation 17–20.

The Millennium

- Why would the reference to one thousand years have come as a surprise to the original audience of Revelation?

  Up until this point, all the references to time in Revelation have been short durations, such as half an hour, an hour, five months, and three and a half years. Moreover, the opening chapter of the book declares that these things shall happen soon. Therefore, first-time readers of this book, accustomed to seeing short periods of time presented, would have been taken aback at the abrupt and unprecedented reference to one thousand years in Revelation 20.

- What two distinct angles on the dragon are presented in Revelation 12 and 20?

  Seen from the angle of Revelation 12, the dragon is strong and successful as it pursues a weak and frail church into the wilderness. Seen from the angle of Revelation 20, the dragon is weak and bound by God, while the church is alive and glorified in Christ. When viewed side by side, Revelation 12 presents the dragon's strength as a brief period of forty-two months, and Revelation 20 presents his containment as a long period of one thousand years.

After the Video

- What three views of the millennium does Dr. Godfrey present? Briefly summarize each.

  The three main views of the millennium are named based on when they believe Christ's return will take place in relation to the period of one thousand years described in Revelation 20. The premillennial view holds that Jesus will return visibly and gloriously before the millennium takes place. Two distinct varieties of premillennialism include historic premillennialism, present among some of the early church fathers, and dispensational premillennialism, which is common among American Protestants today. Postmillennialists believe that Christ will return at the end of the thousand-year period. A third view, often described as amillennialism, argues that the millennium of Revelation 20 refers not to a literal thousand-year period but to the whole history of the church. The millennium is therefore seen as a picture of Christ's reign rather than a period that precedes or follows it.

- How does Revelation 20:1 describe the angel that binds the dragon? Why is this significant?

  Throughout the book of Revelation, John has described heavenly beings in a variety of ways, often using vivid imagery to portray their supernatural characteristics or by describing key angels as "great" angels. However, the angel that performs the momentous task of binding the dragon is described in Revelation 20:1 simply as "an angel." Hence, the power of God is once more displayed in the fact that God's chief antagonist is easily locked away by a relatively ordinary and unremarkable servant of God.

- What is the practical result of the chaining of the dragon for the church's mission today?

  Dr. Godfrey points out that the chaining of the dragon makes the church's mission in the world possible. One of the results of Satan's binding is that he cannot deceive the nations anymore. As a result, Christians can go to the nations and proclaim the gospel successfully. This is a present reality for the church as a result of the ascension and glorification of our Lord that enables us to actually fulfill the Great Commission.

REVIEW QUIZ

Lesson 20

1. **D.**
   The "great supper of God" mentioned in Revelation 19:17 refers to the feast that the carrion birds will enjoy after the last battle when all of God's enemies are defeated. This event symbolizes God's complete victory over the forces of sin and darkness.

2. **B.**
   Revelation 20 is best understood not as an appendix or add-on to the rest of the book but as a critical part of the unfolding message of Revelation. Rather than describing events that take place after the rest of the book, it offers another perspective on the period in which the church now carries out its mission.

3. **D.**
   Most of the church historically has been postmillennial, believing that Christ will return to earth at the end of the millennium described in Revelation 20:1–7.

4. **B.**
   Dispensational premillennialism, a recent theological development, has rapidly expanded from its nineteenth-century origins to become the dominant millennial view among American Protestants today.

5. **A.**
   The abrupt reference to a period of one thousand years in Revelation 20 forms a striking contrast with the very brief periods of time mentioned so far in the book of Revelation. Moreover, references to an eschatological period of one thousand years do not appear anywhere else in Scripture. Therefore, noting the surprise that this would have evoked among Revelation's first readers, Dr. Godfrey argues that the first question to be asked of the text should be "How can there be a thousand years?"

6. **D.**
Mary Slessor was a Scottish missionary who served in Nigeria in the late nineteenth and early twentieth centuries. Although she faced an immense undertaking, she was confident that God would give her enough time to carry out the work entrusted to her. She wrote: "Christ never was in a hurry. There was no rushing forward, no anticipating, no fretting over what might be. Each day's duties were done as each day brought them, and the rest was left with God." Christians can therefore go about the Great Commission with confidence that the work will be finished in accordance with God's appointed time.

21

The Final Judgment

INTRODUCTION

After describing the fall of Babylon, the defeat of the beast, and the chaining of the dragon, John at last turns his attention to the eternal destruction that awaits the dragon in the lake of fire. Not only will God pass judgment on the dragon, but He will also resurrect every person who has ever lived to give an account for their actions. To those whose names appear in the Book of Life He promises an eternity of new life in a new heaven and new earth.

LEARNING GOALS

When you have finished this lesson, you should be able to:

- Describe the future judgment that awaits the dragon and the human race
- Explain how humanity will be judged and what a person must do to be saved

KEY IDEAS

- The ancient dragon, Satan, will be judged by God and will be cast into the lake of fire with all his followers.
- All whose names are written in the Lamb's Book of Life before the foundation of the world will be saved.
- When Jesus returns, He will unite heaven and earth in a glorious new creation.

REFLECTION & DISCUSSION QUESTIONS

Before the Video

What Do You Think?

Take a moment to answer the following questions. They will prepare you for the lecture.

- How will the final judgment take place?

- What do people in our culture think about the notion of future judgment? Should Christians talk with non-Christians about the reality of judgment? Why or why not?

Scripture Reading

> *And just as it is appointed for man to die once, and after that comes judgment, so Christ, having been offered once to bear the sins of many, will appear a second time, not to deal with sin but to save those who are eagerly waiting for him.*
>
> —Hebrews 9:27–28

- According to these verses, what is the difference between Christ's first coming and second coming? What will the result of His second coming be?

During the Video

Answer the following questions while you watch the video. They will guide you through the lecture.

The Judgment of the Dragon *0:00–15:23*

- How does Revelation 20:1–6 offer a picture of the church's strength and victory?

- What is the significance of the reference to Gog and Magog in Revelation 20:8?

The Judgment of Humankind *15:23–19:19*

- On what basis are the dead judged in Revelation 20:12–13?

- What is the primary objective of the reference to the lake of fire in Revelation 20:15?

The Glory after Judgment *19:19–24:17*

- Which does the New Testament describe in greater detail, heaven or the new heaven and the new earth? Explain.

- What is the point of the claim in Revelation 21:1 that there will no longer be any sea?

After the Video

Answer the following questions after you have finished the lecture. They will help you identify and summarize the major points.

- What is Dr. Godfrey's stance toward other interpretations of Revelation 20? What does he fear can happen when we raise unhelpful questions from the text?

  If you are in a group, have the members discuss how their understanding of Revelation has changed or grown during this teaching series. What have you learned that you would most like to share with others?

- What are the contents of the books described in Revelation 20:12? What is the content of the Book of Life? What role do these books play in the final judgment?

  If you are in a group, have the members discuss the description of the final judgment in Revelation 20:11–15. Is this judgment fair or unfair? Explain.

- How are heaven and earth presented in most of Revelation? How does Revelation 21:1–3 redefine the relationship between heaven and earth?

  If you are in a group, have the members answer the following question: Why is it better to spend eternity in a new heaven and a new earth than to spend it in heaven?

PRAYER

Commit what you have learned from God's Word in this lesson to prayer.

- Praise God for His commitment to bring heaven and earth together into a new creation.
- Confess any doubts or discouragement you may have about God's coming victory.
- Thank God for recording the names of His people in the Book of Life before the foundation of the world.
- Ask God to help you share the gospel with others so that others whose names are written in His book will come to believe.

REVIEW QUIZ

Use these multiple-choice questions to measure what you learned from this lesson.

1. What is the "first resurrection" referred to in Revelation 20:6?
   a. The resurrection of Jesus two thousand years ago
   b. The resurrection of the believers' souls in heaven
   c. The resurrection of the saints to eternal life
   d. The resurrection of the ungodly to eternal destruction

2. Which of the following best describes the identity of Gog and Magog in Revelation 20:8?
   a. Babylon
   b. Rome
   c. Unknown future superpower
   d. Vast army of God's enemies

3. Which Bible scholar identified "Jesus wins!" as the central message of Revelation?
   a. Dennis Johnson
   b. G.K. Beale
   c. R.C. Sproul
   d. William Hendriksen

4. When are the names of believers written in the Book of Life?
   a. After they confess Jesus as Savior and Lord
   b. At the moment of their spiritual rebirth
   c. Before the foundation of the world
   d. When they die

5. The New Testament describes what the new heaven and the new earth will be like in far more abundant detail than it uses to describe what heaven will be like.
   a. True
   b. False

6. The Old Testament covenant promise is most powerfully reasserted in which of the following descriptions of the new heaven and the new earth?
   a. All things will be made new.
   b. God will be with them and will be their God.
   c. There will be no more death, mourning, crying, or pain.
   d. There will no longer be any sea.

Answer Key—The Final Judgment

REFLECTION & DISCUSSION QUESTIONS

Before the Video

What Do You Think?

These are personal questions. The answers should be based on your own knowledge and experience.

Scripture Reading

- According to these verses, what is the difference between Christ's first coming and second coming? What will the result of His second coming be?

  Hebrews 9:27–28 identifies the purpose of Christ's first coming as bearing the sins of many and the purpose of His second coming as saving "those who are eagerly waiting for him." The result of His second coming will therefore include the judgment of all humanity, which will result in the final act of the salvation of His people.

During the Video

The Judgment of the Dragon

- How does Revelation 20:1–6 offer a picture of the church's strength and victory?

  In Revelation 20:1–6, it is not just Jesus who reigns over the whole world but Jesus and His departed saints. Christians who have departed this life are now in heaven with God, beholding Christ and entering into His triumph. Although they were once downtrodden and oppressed in this life, they are now reigning and rejoicing in the presence of their King.

- What is the significance of the reference to Gog and Magog in Revelation 20:8?

  Revelation 20:8 reports that in the final battle God's enemies will gather from all corners of the earth, from Gog and Magog, to wage war against the Lord. This reference to Gog and Magog comes from Ezekiel 38–39, where Gog and Magog refer to enemies of Israel that will gather against the Lord's people and be defeated by the power of God. Therefore, this reference is intended to remind God's people of His ancient promise to defend them against an overwhelming force and to present His future victory in a similar light.

The Judgment of Humankind

- On what basis are the dead judged in Revelation 20:12–13?

  Revelation 20 indicates that the dead will be judged on the basis of what they have done. Because all have sinned and fall short of God's righteous standard, to be judged on the basis of one's works is to be found worthy of eternal punishment. The only way to avoid this punishment is to have one's name written in the Book of Life.

- What is the primary objective of the reference to the lake of fire in Revelation 20:15?

  John's summary of the final judgment concludes with the statement that all whose names are not written in the Book of Life will be cast into the lake of fire. This reference to eternal punishment as a lake of fire is likely symbolic and therefore is not intended to describe the physical nature of that eternal punishment. Instead, its primary objective is to issue a plea for all people to repent of their sins and find new life in Christ.

The Glory after Judgment

- Which does the New Testament describe in greater detail, heaven or the new heaven and the new earth? Explain.

  Although heaven is mentioned throughout the New Testament, it is rarely described. Christians are informed that heaven is a wonderful place where God's people will experience rest in the presence of the Lord, but we know very little about what heaven will be like. On the other hand, the final chapters of Revelation offer a wealth of information about the new heaven and the new earth, where believers will live with the Lord forever.

- What is the point of the claim in Revelation 21:1 that there will no longer be any sea?

  Going all the way back to the creation narrative in Genesis 1, the sea is associated with formlessness and chaos. Throughout the history of Old Testament Israel, the sea continued to symbolize chaos and destruction, which is why the beast is associated with the sea in Revelation 12:17. The pronouncement that there will no longer be any sea in the new heaven and new earth is less of a claim about the geography of the new earth and more of a claim about the removal of chaos and destruction from God's created order.

After the Video

- What is Dr. Godfrey's stance toward other interpretations of Revelation 20? What does he fear can happen when we raise unhelpful questions from the text?

  While reflecting on the dramatically different ways that Christians interpret Revelation 20, Dr. Godfrey remarks that he has no desire to fight over other interpretations of Revelation 20 or to be contentious about his interpretation of God's Word. At the same time, he expresses his fear that Christians often raise bizarre questions that don't really apply to Revelation's message and consequently miss the point and the blessing that God desires to communicate through this book. Rather than draw misguided conclusions from the text, Dr. Godfrey wants

Christians to be encouraged that we are reigning with Christ now, that we have plenty of time to carry out Christ's mission, and that the devil will be thwarted in his efforts to defy God and destroy the church.

- What are the contents of the books described in Revelation 20:12? What is the content of the Book of Life? What role do these books play in the final judgment?

  The books that are opened in Revelation 20:12 contain records of the deeds of all human beings. In contrast, the Book of Life simply contains the names of those who belong to Jesus Christ. All whose names are listed in the Book of Life will experience the joy of the new heaven and the new earth. All whose names do not appear in the Book of Life will be judged on the basis of their deeds recorded in the other books. Because no one can attain God's righteous standard, those judged on the basis of their own works will be found guilty and will be thrown into the lake of fire.

- How are heaven and earth presented in most of Revelation? How does Revelation 21:1–3 redefine the relationship between heaven and earth?

  Revelation consistently presents a contrast between heaven and earth. Those who dwell in heaven are the saved; those who dwell on earth are the lost. Heaven is the heavenly temple where God, the angels, and the redeemed are found; earth is the place of the dragon, the beast, and Babylon. Throughout Revelation, the narrative shifts back and forth between heaven and earth. In Revelation 21, that separation between earth and heaven comes to an end. The heavenly Jerusalem that has existed in glory will become visible and will remake the whole earth and all of its character in accordance with God's beauty and perfection. Best of all, God Himself will come to dwell among His people and will be with them as their God.

REVIEW QUIZ

Lesson 21

1. **B.**
   The "first resurrection" in Revelation 20:6 refers not to the physical resurrection of the bodies of believers at the last day but to the spiritual life and glory that believers will experience in heaven before Christ's return.

2. **D.**
   The reference to Gog and Magog is not intended to associate the dragon's army with any particular nation but rather alludes to the vast army of Israel's enemies that God vanquished in Ezekiel 38–39.

3. **A.**
   Dr. Godfrey's friend and colleague Dr. Dennis Johnson summarized the book of Revelation by saying: "What's the book of Revelation all about? Jesus wins!" This statement accurately summarizes the central message of this book.

4. **C.**
   Revelation 13:8 records that the names of God's people who will not worship the beast were written in the Lamb's Book of Life before the foundation of the world. This verse, coupled with the description of the Book of Life in Revelation 20, bears beautiful witness to the doctrine of election.

5. **A.**
   Although heaven is mentioned frequently throughout the New Testament, few details are given about what heaven will be like. On the other hand, a very detailed description of the new heaven and new earth appears in Revelation 21–22.

6. **B.**
   The very heart of the Old Testament covenant is that God will be in our midst, that He will be our God, and that we will be His people. This covenant promise is powerfully reaffirmed in the promise of Revelation 21:3: "Behold, the dwelling place of God is with man. He will dwell with them, and they will be his people, and God himself will be with them as their God."

22

The New Jerusalem

INTRODUCTION

After describing Christ's ultimate victory over the dragon, the beast, and rebellious humanity, John turns his attention to the glorious future that awaits all those whose names are written in the Lamb's Book of Life. As we survey the final chapters of Revelation, we encounter lofty descriptions and otherworldly imagery that our finite minds can barely fathom. Though John tells us many things that we cannot yet understand, he nevertheless offers us the clear and beautiful hope of a day that is quickly coming when God will dwell with us and we will be His people.

LEARNING GOALS

When you have finished this lesson, you should be able to:

- Describe what the new Jerusalem will be like
- Identify and explain key symbols that John uses to communicate the wonders of the heavenly city

KEY IDEAS

- In the new Jerusalem, Christians will enjoy liberation from all the effects of the fall.
- Jesus Christ, the Lord of history, will consummate His kingdom and make all things new.
- God's people will experience perfect communion with a perfect God in a perfect city for all eternity.

REFLECTION & DISCUSSION QUESTIONS

Before the Video

What Do You Think?

Take a moment to answer the following questions. They will prepare you for the lecture.

- What do you imagine that a new, perfect earth will be like? What do you look forward to about a new life in a new world with a new body?

- When you think about being in God's presence, what excites you? What terrifies you?

Scripture Reading

But you have come to Mount Zion and to the city of the living God, the heavenly Jerusalem, and to innumerable angels in festal gathering, and to the assembly of the firstborn who are enrolled in heaven, and to God, the judge of all, and to the spirits of the righteous made perfect, and to Jesus, the mediator of a new covenant, and to the sprinkled blood that speaks a better word than the blood of Abel. . . . Therefore let us be grateful for receiving a kingdom that cannot be shaken, and thus let us offer to God acceptable worship, with reverence and awe, for our God is a consuming fire.

—Hebrews 12:22–24, 28–29

- How is the heavenly Jerusalem described in this passage? On what basis do believers gain access to this heavenly city?

During the Video

Answer the following questions while you watch the video. They will guide you through the lecture.

Overview of the New Jerusalem *0:00–14:17*

- What are the three primary effects of humanity's fall into sin?

- What is the connection between the list of sins in Revelation 21:8 and the letters to the seven churches?

- How does Dr. Godfrey describe the symbolism of Revelation 21:9–27?

Twelve Characteristics of the New Jerusalem *14:17–23:01*

- Briefly list the twelve characteristics of the new Jerusalem that Dr. Godfrey identifies in this lesson.

- How does the future new Jerusalem contrast with the present state of this world?

After the Video

Answer the following questions after you have finished the lecture. They will help you identify and summarize the major points.

- How should Christians understand the dimensions of the new Jerusalem as described in Revelation 21:16?

  If you are in a group, have the members read John 14:2–3. What blessing and encouragement do these verses offer to you?

- Why will there be no temple in the new Jerusalem? How does this fit into the larger framework of the biblical story?

  If you are in a group, have the members describe the importance of God's presence in their lives. What do you think about dwelling in a place where God is present all the time?

- What is significant about the absence of the sun, the moon, and night in the new Jerusalem?

  If you are in a group, have the members read Psalm 36:9. How does this verse reinforce the main idea of Revelation 21:23–24?

PRAYER

Commit what you have learned from God's Word in this lesson to prayer.

- Praise God for creating a perfect city where He will dwell with humanity forever.
- Confess areas of temptation where Jesus invites you to repent and overcome.

- Thank God for the certainty of a glorious eternal dwelling place.
- Ask God to help you fix your eyes on Christ and on His imperishable kingdom.

REVIEW QUIZ

Use these multiple-choice questions to measure what you learned from this lesson.

1. Which of the three effects of the fall can be fully taken away in this life?
   a. Individual corruption before God
   b. Individual guilt before God
   c. Earth's subjection to misery and brokenness
   d. None of the above

2. According to Dr. Godfrey, how does Jesus present Himself in Revelation 21:5–8?
   a. Lamb who was slain
   b. Light of the world
   c. Lion of Judah
   d. Lord of history

3. Which Reformed scholar once teased Dr. Godfrey for not knowing how to pronounce the names of the jewels in Revelation 21:19–20?
   a. Dennis E. Johnson
   b. G.K. Beale
   c. James Montgomery Boice
   d. R.C. Sproul

4. Who builds the new Jerusalem?
   a. Angels
   b. Christians
   c. God
   d. Kings of the earth

5. The names written on the gates and foundations of the walls in the new Jerusalem demonstrate the unity of Israel and the church.
   a. True
   b. False

6. What is the length of the new Jerusalem?
   a. 12 miles
   b. 1,000 cubits
   c. 1,400 miles
   d. 7,000 stadia

Answer Key—The New Jerusalem

REFLECTION & DISCUSSION QUESTIONS

Before the Video

What Do You Think?

These are personal questions. The answers should be based on your own knowledge and experience.

Scripture Reading

- How is the heavenly Jerusalem described in this passage? On what basis do believers gain access to this heavenly city?

  Hebrews 12 describes the heavenly Jerusalem as a kingdom that cannot be shaken, the city of the living God, the site of Mount Zion, and of the joyous assembly of thousands of angels and of the saints who have been redeemed and perfected by Christ. This passage also describes Jesus as the Mediator. By His blood, the saints are redeemed, purified, and set apart to be God's holy people.

During the Video

Overview of the New Jerusalem

- What are the three primary effects of humanity's fall into sin?

  Theologians typically identify three main effects of the fall. First, humanity has become guilty before God. Second, humanity has become corrupt before God. Third, humanity now lives in a misery-bound world that has been warped by the effects of sin. The first two effects of the fall are personal and individual. Christ has resolved our guilt by making atonement for our sins on the cross. Christ is resolving our corruption by sanctifying us through the indwelling of His Holy Spirit. Christ will resolve the misery and brokenness of the world when He returns to make all things new.

- What is the connection between the list of sins in Revelation 21:8 and the letters to the seven churches?

  Revelation 21:8 presents a list of sins that characterize those who will not enter the new Jerusalem. Interestingly, these sins correspond with the sins mentioned in the letters to the seven churches in Revelation 2–3. Revelation 21:8 therefore reveals the eternal fate of those who do not overcome but who succumb to the pressures and temptations of this life, revealing that their names have not been written in the Lamb's Book of Life. The appearance of these sins in the letters to the churches also shows that these sins present a temptation to believers and unbelievers alike. Christians can take heart that they need not be defined by those sins but have the opportunity in Christ to overcome and enter into the splendor of the new Jerusalem.

- How does Dr. Godfrey describe the symbolism of Revelation 21:9–27?

  Dr. Godfrey identified a variety of rich symbolism in the description of the new Jerusalem found in Revelation 21:9–27. Though we do not know the color or characteristics of all the jewels described in verses 19–20, they nevertheless present a picture of glory, beauty, and strength. The description of a gate made out of pearl in verse 21 presents not an actual, physical, giant pearl but a symbol of splendor that surpasses anything found in this world. The gold that is clear as crystal in verse 18 is meant to describe a purity and brilliance that transcend the purest gold that we can fathom. All in all, the rich and splendid descriptions in this passage are meant to convey a place so great and wonderful that we can only begin to imagine it.

Twelve Characteristics of the New Jerusalem

- Briefly list the twelve characteristics of the new Jerusalem that Dr. Godfrey identifies in this lesson.

  In the second half of this lecture, Dr. Godfrey identified the following twelve characteristics of the new Jerusalem: (1) it is a gift of God, (2) it manifests the very glory of God, (3) it is precious and valuable, (4) it is beautiful, (5) it is safe, (6) it is a place for all the people of God, (7) it is huge, (8) it incorporates beauty and value together, (9) it has no temple, (10) it does not have sun, moon, or night, (11) it is where kings will bring their glory to serve the Lord, and (12) it is holy.

- How does the future new Jerusalem contrast with the present state of this world?

  Dr. Godfrey closed this lesson by noting the striking contrast between the promised new Jerusalem and the present conditions of this world. Christians live in a sad and dying world where everything passes away and even the best and most glorious things in life are subject to decay. In contrast, God promises believers a future city of life and light that will endure forever and resonate with the holy presence of God among His people.

After the Video

- How should Christians understand the dimensions of the new Jerusalem described in Revelation 21:16?

  Like many other details in this passage, the dimensions of the new Jerusalem are best understood symbolically. The city is described as a vast cube that is 1,400 miles wide, deep, and high. This description creates a picture of the heavenly city that is perfectly balanced, symmetrical, and orderly and that offers abundant space to all who dwell there.

- Why will there be no temple in the new Jerusalem? How does this fit into the larger framework of the biblical story?

  Throughout the Bible, the temple is both a place where God chooses to be present and a symbol for His presence. A temple will not be needed in the new Jerusalem because God Himself will be there. Moreover, the temple also represents moral and physical separation between sinful people and a holy God. Because Christians will be completely glorified and free of their present moral corruption, they will have direct, unmediated access to God. In the new Jerusalem, there will no longer be any distance or separation from God because He will surround Himself with a people whom He has made holy.

- What is significant about the absence of the sun, the moon, and night in the new Jerusalem?

  Revelation 21:23–24 expresses the idea that the new Jerusalem will have no need of sun, moon, day, or night because God Himself will be the light in the midst of His people. This is likely a symbolic statement of God's surpassing greatness and beauty in comparison with all created things. Instead of looking up at the sun and admiring its beauty, God's people will behold their glorious God and find that His presence illuminates every aspect of their lives.

REVIEW QUIZ

Lesson 22

1. **B.**
   Of the three main effects of the fall, only individual guilt before God can be dealt with fully in this life. When we place our faith in Christ, God imputes our guilty record to Christ and imputes His sinless record to us. Therefore, Christians are morally blameless before God. However, the lingering effects of sin, seen individually in our sinful nature and universally in the misery of a fallen world, will not be rectified until we are glorified and the world is made new.

2. **D.**
   Dr. Godfrey notes that Jesus presents Himself in Revelation 21:5–8 as the Lord of history. He is the Alpha and Omega, the beginning and the end. He has opened the scroll of human history and consummated the eternal purposes of the Father.

3. **D.**
   In this lesson, Dr. Godfrey shared a story in which he read a portion of Revelation 21 out loud at a conference and skipped over the names of the jewels because he did not know how to pronounce them. Dr. Sproul, who spoke after Dr. Godfrey, playfully teased him for doing that.

4. **C.**
   The first characteristic of the new Jerusalem that Dr. Godfrey pointed out is the fact that the city is a gift of God. It is a city that God builds and that descends from heaven as God's gift to the redeemed human race.

5. **A.**
   The gates of the heavenly city display the names of the twelve tribes of Israel, and the foundations of the walls display the names of the twelve Apostles. These architectural features of the city reveal that it is the dwelling place for Israel and the church, the whole people of God.

6. **C.**
   The new Jerusalem is described as a cube that is 12,000 stadia—approximately 1,400 miles—in length, width, and height. These dimensions are symbols that communicate the perfect order, balance, and symmetry of this vast city.

23

Come, Lord Jesus

INTRODUCTION

As we approach the end of our survey of the book of Revelation, we will reflect on major themes of John's conclusion to this book and major themes of Revelation as a whole. Dr. Godfrey powerfully paraphrases this book's final message to its readers: "God is more glorious than you think. Life is not what you see. Life is not even what you think. It's always better. God is more glorious. Sin is more serious. Evil is more powerful, suffering is greater, time is shorter, and Jesus is stronger."

LEARNING GOALS

When you have finished this lesson, you should be able to:

- Explain the significance of the final scene in Revelation's seventh cycle
- Describe the literary structure and main ideas of the conclusion to the book of Revelation

KEY IDEAS

- Jesus truly is returning soon.
- Jesus invites all who are thirsty to come to Him and drink the water of life.
- Jesus has given Revelation to His people as a book of blessing and encouragement while we await His glorious return.

REFLECTION & DISCUSSION QUESTIONS

Before the Video

What Do You Think?

Take a moment to answer the following questions. They will prepare you for the lecture.

- What things in your life or in the world cause you to cry out, "Come, Lord Jesus"?

- Is it important to have the expectation that Jesus is coming soon? Why or why not?

- How does the promise of Christ's sudden return prompt you to live differently?

Scripture Reading

But do not overlook this one fact, beloved, that with the Lord one day is as a thousand years, and a thousand years as one day. The Lord is not slow to fulfill his promise as some count slowness, but is patient toward you, not wishing that any should perish, but that all should reach repentance. But the day of the Lord will come like a thief, and then the heavens will pass away with a roar, and the heavenly bodies will be burned up and dissolved, and the earth and the works that are done on it will be exposed. Since all these things are thus to be dissolved, what sort of people ought you to be in lives of holiness and godliness, waiting for and hastening the coming of the day of God, because of which the heavens will be set on fire and dissolved, and the heavenly bodies will melt as they burn! But according to his promise we are waiting for new heavens and a new earth in which righteousness dwells. Therefore, beloved, since you are waiting for these, be diligent to be found by him without spot or blemish, and at peace.

—2 Peter 3:8–14

- How does Peter describe God's approach to time? Why has Jesus not yet returned? What does Peter encourage believers to do as they await Christ's return?

During the Video

Answer the following questions while you watch the video. They will guide you through the lecture.

The River and the Tree *0:00–4:54*

- Which symbols from the Bible are pulled together in Revelation 22:1–5?

- To what Old Testament passages does the description of the tree on both sides of the river in Revelation 22:1–5 allude?

John's Conclusion *4:54–21:27*

- What is the chiastic structure of the conclusion to the book of Revelation?

- To whom is the invitation to come in Revelation 22:17 addressed? What is the significance of this appeal?

- What warning is issued in Revelation 22:18–19? What other parallel warnings appear in this passage?

After the Video

Answer the following questions after you have finished the lecture. They will help you identify and summarize the major points.

- What does Dr. Godfrey propose as a possible summary of the book of Revelation? How would you summarize this book?

  If you are in a group, have the members identify and share what they consider to be the most important themes from the book of Revelation.
- According to Dr. Godfrey, if the main points of Revelation are so simple and clear, why does the book of Revelation need to be so complicated? Do you agree or disagree?

  If you are in a group, have the members discuss which of the reasons above they find most convincing.
- Dr. Godfrey began this teaching series by describing Revelation as a book of blessing. How have you been blessed during this study of the book of Revelation?

  If you are in a group, have the members share specific ways that they have been blessed as a result of this focused study of the book of Revelation.

PRAYER

Commit what you have learned from God's Word in this lesson to prayer.

- Praise God for giving Revelation, this book of blessing, to His church.
- Confess anything that holds you back from coming to Jesus, the living water, to quench your every thirst.

- Thank God for His presence with His people throughout all generations.
- Ask, "Come, Lord Jesus!"

REVIEW QUIZ

Use these multiple-choice questions to measure what you learned from this lesson.

1. Throughout Scripture, trees routinely symbolize all *except* which of the following?
   a. Fruitfulness
   b. Knowledge
   c. Life
   d. Stability
2. What forms the center of the literary chiasm in Revelation 22:6–21?
   a. Appeal
   b. Blessing
   c. Promise
   d. Warning
3. Which of the following best summarizes the overall message of Revelation?
   a. "Come, Lord Jesus!"
   b. "Do not seal up the words of the prophecy of this book."
   c. "These words are trustworthy and true."
   d. "Worship God."
4. Who is invited to "come" in Revelation 22:17?
   a. The bride of Christ
   b. The Lord Jesus
   c. The one who is thirsty
   d. The Spirit
5. What punishment is promised to those who add to the words of Revelation?
   a. God will add to them the mark of the beast.
   b. God will take away their share in the Tree of Life.
   c. Their lampstand will be removed.
   d. They will experience the plagues described in this book.
6. Which of the following does Revelation *not* call on Christians to do?
   a. Build the new Jerusalem
   b. Conquer in faith
   c. Live faithfully for Christ
   d. Persevere

Answer Key—Come, Lord Jesus

REFLECTION & DISCUSSION QUESTIONS

Before the Video

What Do You Think?

These are personal questions. The answers should be based on your own knowledge and experience.

Scripture Reading

- How does Peter describe God's approach to time? Why has Jesus not yet returned? What does Peter encourage believers to do as they await Christ's return?

  Writing to believers who were confronting questions about why Jesus had not yet returned, Peter points out that God's approach to time is different from theirs. In God's timing a day is as one thousand years and vice versa. Peter also affirms that God does not delay in keeping His promises but instead is allowing more time for the full number of His people to come to faith. In light of their eagerness for Christ's return, Peter encourages these believers to conduct themselves in holiness, godliness, and peace, being without blemish and diligent to be found in Christ.

During the Video

The River and the Tree

- Which symbols from the Bible are pulled together in Revelation 22:1–5?

  This passage ties together symbols from throughout Scripture, including the tree of life, the throne of God, the water-like crystal that flows forth from God's presence, the use of the number twelve to represent the completion of God's people, God's name like a mark on the foreheads of His people, and verdant imagery that describes the flourishing of God's people.

- To what Old Testament passages does the description of the tree on both sides of the river in Revelation 22:1–5 allude?

  Revelation 22:1–5, with its powerful picture of the Tree of Life on both sides of the river, alludes to a variety of Old Testament passages. First is Genesis 2:9, where the original Tree of Life appears in the garden of Eden. This passage also evokes imagery of Psalm 1:3 and Psalm 92:12, which describe the flourishing of God's people in terms of healthy, well-watered trees that yield abundant fruit. Also alluded to in this passage is Ezekiel 47:12, where verdant, healthy trees grow on both sides of the river that flows out from the temple.

John's Conclusion

- What is the chiastic structure of the conclusion to the book of Revelation?

  Dr. Godfrey identified a chiastic structure to the conclusion of this book. This chiasm consists of five elements. The outer layer of the chiasm is formed by an opening promise and blessing in 22:6–7 and a closing promise and blessing in 22:20–21. Next, the inner layer of the chiasm contains a first warning in 22:8–16 and a second warning in 22:18–19. An evangelistic appeal in 22:17 forms the center of this chiasm.

- To whom is the invitation to come in Revelation 22:17 addressed? What is the significance of this appeal?

  The invitation to come in Revelation 22:17, expressed by the Spirit, the bride, and all who receive the record of John's vision, is addressed to any who are thirsty and desire to drink of the water of life. This appeal is significant because it stands at the chiastic center of the conclusion to Revelation. Furthermore, it represents the great evangelistic call of a book that does not otherwise have a prominent evangelistic focus.

- What warning is issued in Revelation 22:18–19? What other parallel warnings appear in this passage?

  Revelation 22:18–19 warns that if anyone adds to the words of this book, God will add to him the plagues described in it. If anyone takes away from the words of this book, God will take away the blessings described in it (i.e., the Tree of Life and the new Jerusalem). This serious warning highlights the severity of tampering with God's revelation to His people. Parallel warnings in this passage include exhortations to faithful worship, faithful living, and trusting in Jesus. These verses indicate that keeping Scripture intact is on the same moral level as worshiping God correctly, following in His path correctly, and believing in Jesus correctly.

After the Video

- What does Dr. Godfrey propose as a possible summary of the book of Revelation? How would you summarize this book?

  Dr. Godfrey noted that the overall message of this book is clear and has been repeated throughout the book. He noted that a possible summary of this book could be "Worship God, be holy, avoid the judgment, and trust Jesus to be Savior."

- According to Dr. Godfrey, if the main points of Revelation are so simple and clear, why does the book of Revelation need to be so complicated? Do you agree or disagree?

  Even though the basic message of Revelation is very simple, Dr. Godfrey argued that there are good reasons why this book communicates a simple message in complicated ways. The first reason is to prompt readers to slow down, ponder, and reflect on this book. The second reason is to show us that God delights to communicate to His people in a variety of different ways and different genres that connect differently with different types of people. The third reason is that God sometimes prefers to communicate His truth to us in ways that are particularly vivid, memorable, and arresting. By speaking to us in this way, God imparts powerful pictures and metaphors that speak to us more eloquently than straightforward propositional statements.

- Dr. Godfrey began this teaching series by describing Revelation as a book of blessing. How have you been blessed during this study of the book of Revelation?

  Answers to this question are personal and will vary from person to person.

REVIEW QUIZ

Lesson 23

1. **B.**

   Trees often appear throughout Scripture as symbols of life, stability, and fruitfulness. Although the Tree of Knowledge of Good and Evil features prominently in Genesis 2–3, the use of a tree to symbolize knowledge is rare in the rest of the Bible.

2. **A.**

   The chiastic structure of Revelation's conclusion includes a promise and blessing as the outer layers, a warning as the inner layer, and an evangelistic appeal at the very center.

3. **D.**

   Dr. Godfrey argued that the angel's words to John, "Worship God," accurately summarize the underlying message of the book of Revelation. While this book is intended to impart knowledge and understanding, its principal aim is to motivate God's people to worship God, overcome suffering, and trust in Jesus.

4. **C.**

   Revelation 22:17, with its invitation for the thirsty to come and take the water of life without price, represents the great evangelistic appeal of Revelation to trust in Christ.

5. **D.**

   In Revelation 22:18, Jesus warns that anyone who adds to the words of this book will also have the plagues described in this book added to him.

6. **A.**

   In the previous lesson, Dr. Godfrey noted that the new Jerusalem is a gift from God, not built by God's people. At the end of this lesson, Dr. Godfrey made the observation that Revelation is a book of pastoral encouragement that God's people might be faithful, might persevere, and might conquer in faith, knowing that Jesus is returning soon.

24

Questions Answered

INTRODUCTION

Even though the basic message of Revelation is simple enough for any Christian to understand, a lifetime is still not long enough to learn everything that this book has to offer. In this final lesson, Dr. Godfrey turns his attention to common questions that arise from studying this book. Whether all your questions are answered or not, his hope is that you have been richly blessed through this study of Revelation and that you will continue to be blessed as you seek to know Christ and to make Him known to others.

LEARNING GOALS

When you have finished this lesson, you should be able to:

- Express a greater sense of familiarity with the book of Revelation
- Navigate some of the questions that frequently arise in the study of this book
- Continue asking deep questions as you progress in your study of God's Word

KEY IDEAS

- A responsible approach to the Bible's prophetic and apocalyptic literature allows each book to speak for itself without adopting a "cut and paste" approach to Scripture.
- Descriptions of judgment in the Bible should fill Christians with compassion and motivate them both to proclaim the gospel and to try to alleviate human suffering.
- Because Christians will arrive at differing interpretations of Revelation, humility and grace are essential when seeking to understand this book.

REFLECTION & DISCUSSION QUESTIONS

Before the Video

What Do You Think?

Take a moment to answer the following questions. They will prepare you for the lecture.

- What have you enjoyed most about your study of the book of Revelation? What is one of the most important things you have learned during this study?

- What lesson or truth from the book of Revelation do people most need to hear? Explain.

Scripture Reading

"I, Jesus, have sent my angel to testify to you about these things for the churches. I am the root and the descendant of David, the bright morning star." The Spirit and the Bride say, "Come." And let the one who hears say, "Come." And let the one who is thirsty come; let the one who desires take the water of life without price. I warn everyone who hears the words of the prophecy of this book: if anyone adds to them, God will add to him the plagues described in this book, and if anyone takes away from the words of the book of this prophecy, God will take away his share in the tree of life and in the holy city, which are described in this book. He who testifies to these things says, "Surely I am coming soon." Amen. Come, Lord Jesus! The grace of the Lord Jesus be with all. Amen.

—Revelation 22:16–21

- How is Jesus presented in these verses? What promises or blessings are extended to the reader in this passage?

During the Video

Answer the following questions while you watch the video. They will guide you through the lecture.

Biblical Prophecy: General or Specific? *0:00–7:17*

- What is the difference between prophetic books and apocalyptic books?

- How does a person arrive at the conclusion that there will be a rapture and a seven-year tribulation? How does that approach to Scripture differ from the approach Dr. Godfrey has taken?

Addressing Popular Misconceptions *7:17–22:46*

- Why do some interpreters conclude that the number of the beast refers to Nero? What does Dr. Godfrey think of this theory?
- When was the book of Revelation most likely written? How would the dating of Revelation influence its interpretation?
- How does Dr. Godfrey's view of the 144,000 compare to the way Jehovah's Witnesses understand that number?

After the Video

Answer the following questions after you have finished the lecture. They will help you identify and summarize the major points.

- Is it accurate or helpful to identify specific instances of human suffering with God's judgment in Revelation? How should Christians respond to suffering that seems to be the result of that person's wrongdoing?

  If you are in a group, have the members identify and share what they consider to be the most important biblical principles for responding to pain and suffering.
- Is the current nation of Israel a fulfillment of biblical prophecy? Why or why not?

  If you are in a group, have the members discuss the relationship between prophecy and current events. Should Christians expect to see the events of Revelation unfolding in the news today? Why or why not?
- As you reflect on your experience in studying the book of Revelation in this twenty-four-part teaching series, what concepts, verses, or passages have most significantly shaped your understanding of this book? How is Jesus calling you to live differently as a result of this study?

  If you are in a group, have the members discuss their answers to the above questions and discuss what questions they still have about Revelation and the end times.

PRAYER

Commit what you have learned from God's Word in this lesson to prayer.

- Praise God for giving the book of Revelation with its wealth of beauty, truth, and encouragement to His church.
- Confess changes that you need to make in your life as a result of Revelation's call to repentance, purity, and faithfulness.
- Thank God for His church throughout the ages and around the world, which has been faithful to overcome great trials and suffering for the sake of Jesus.
- Ask God to help you approach the future with renewed hopefulness and confidence in your risen and returning King.

REVIEW QUIZ

Use these multiple-choice questions to measure what you learned from this lesson.

1. Which of the following approaches is most helpful for interpreting apocalyptic literature?
   a. Identifying specific people, places, and things to which symbols refer
   b. Focusing on the literal meaning of every word
   c. Reading a specific verse in light of the flow of thought around it
   d. Weaving verses from different passages together to find a new meaning

2. Which of the following psalms describes God's relationship to time in terms similar to those in 2 Peter 3:8?
   a. Psalm 1:3
   b. Psalm 63:1–3
   c. Psalm 90:4
   d. Psalm 136:1

3. It is more accurate to describe the experience of believers after death as everlasting life than as eternal life.
   a. True
   b. False

4. Orthodox Jews consider the current state of Israel to be a fulfillment of biblical prophecy.
   a. True
   b. False

5. Which of the following best describes Revelation's main focus when it portrays wars between the forces of God and Satan?
   a. The length of the struggle
   b. The primary tactics used by each side
   c. The timing of the battles
   d. The victorious nature of God and His people

6. According to Dr. Godfrey, what is the current state of unbelievers as they await the final judgment?
   a. Everlasting torment
   b. Intermediate state of suffering
   c. Peace and happiness
   d. Unconsciousness

Answer Key—Questions Answered

REFLECTION & DISCUSSION QUESTIONS

Before the Video

What Do You Think?

These are personal questions. The answers should be based on your own knowledge and experience.

Scripture Reading

- How is Jesus presented in these verses? What promises or blessings are extended to the reader in this passage?

  In these verses, Jesus describes Himself in messianic terms as the root, the descendant of David, and the morning star. He states that He is the One who has sent His angel to share the testimony of Revelation with John. Therefore, this book is not only a revelation about Jesus Christ but also a revelation from Jesus Christ. Significantly, the final words of Jesus recorded in the entire canon of Scripture are "Surely I am coming soon."

  In addition to the promise that Jesus is coming soon, these verses also include an invitation for all who are thirsty to come and drink from the water of life. Finally, John concludes this book by extending a parting blessing to his readers: "The grace of the Lord Jesus be with all."

During the Video

Biblical Prophecy: General or Specific?

- What is the difference between prophetic books and apocalyptic books?

  Prophetic books, such as Isaiah, Jeremiah, Ezekiel, and the Minor Prophets, tend to include very specific prophecies directed to certain nations or groups at particular times. For instance, when God instructs a prophet to deliver a prophecy against Babylon or Edom, interpreters can confidently associate that prophecy with a specific nation that existed in history. Apocalyptic literature, on the other hand, is less specific. Revelation, along with the latter portion of Daniel, exhibits the tendency of apocalyptic literature to rely more heavily on symbols and imagery in speaking to a broader context instead of one specific group of people at one specific point in time.

- How does a person arrive at the conclusion that there will be a rapture and a seven-year tribulation? How does that approach to Scripture differ from the approach Dr. Godfrey has taken?

Dr. Godfrey pointed out that interpreters of Revelation who argue strongly for a rapture, a seven-year tribulation, and a literal millennium rely on an exegetical approach that moves rapidly back and forth from Revelation to Daniel to Isaiah to Matthew, taking half a verse here and connecting it to a verse there. A major problem with this kind of cut-and-paste approach to Scripture is that it ignores the literary cohesion and flow of thought of each of these books and tends to force conclusions upon them instead of allowing them to speak for themselves. Dr. Godfrey instead attempts to focus on Revelation as a distinct literary unit and interpret it based on its own literary structure and thematic presentation.

Addressing Popular Misconceptions

- Why do some interpreters conclude that the number of the beast refers to Nero? What does Dr. Godfrey think of this theory?

  Interpreters of Revelation who use the technique known as gematria and who desire to situate Revelation in its first-century context have often concluded that the number of the beast refers to Nero. By assigning numeric value to Nero's full name in a certain way, it is possible to yield 666 as the numeric value of his name. So, while Dr. Godfrey noted that it is possible that Nero could be referred to in Revelation 13:18, he is not convinced that Nero fills the full meaning of that image. Even if Nero represented a partial manifestation of the beast in the first century, Christians today and in every century experience the beast's fury in ways that go far beyond Nero.

- When was the book of Revelation most likely written? How would the dating of Revelation influence its interpretation?

  Most conservative scholars believe that Revelation was written after the destruction of the temple in AD 70. Whether Revelation was written before or after the destruction of the temple actually makes no difference to Dr. Godfrey's interpretation of the book. However, this issue is important to preterists, who argue that Revelation is prophesying the destruction of the temple and must therefore have been written before AD 70.

- How does Dr. Godfrey's view of the 144,000 compare to the way Jehovah's Witnesses understand that number?

  Jehovah's Witnesses understand the 144,000 of Revelation as referring to a literal group of 144,000 people who will be the most blessed, in contrast with the rest of the saved, who will experience less blessing in the afterlife. Dr. Godfrey disagreed with this view and instead affirmed that 144,000 is best understood as a symbolic number that refers to the totality of God's redeemed people.

After the Video

- Is it accurate or helpful to identify specific instances of human suffering with God's judgment in Revelation? How should Christians respond to suffering that seems to be the result of that person's wrongdoing?

Because the plagues and judgment described in Revelation occur throughout human history, there is some general truth to the idea that certain natural disasters and calamities that take place today are part of God's overall judgment against a sinful world. However, it is difficult and dangerous to try to identify a clear correlation between the actions of certain groups of people and the misfortunes that they experience. Furthermore, it is wrong for Christians to withhold aid from those who are suffering by rationalizing that suffering as divine judgment. Instead, a biblical approach to suffering—whether it is linked to wrongdoing or not—is to demonstrate the love of Christ through our actions as we also proclaim the gospel of Christ with our words.

- Is the current nation of Israel a fulfillment of biblical prophecy? Why or why not?

  Dr. Godfrey, along with most Reformed scholars and the Orthodox Jewish community, does not believe that the current state of Israel is a fulfillment of biblical prophecy. It is difficult to identify a clear prophecy in the New Testament that would support that conclusion. Instead, the vision of future hope for the Jews expressed in passages like Romans 11 is for the eventual conversion of Jews to Christianity and not for the establishment of a political state.

- As you reflect on your experience studying the book of Revelation in this twenty-four-part teaching series, what concepts, verses, or passages have most significantly shaped your understanding of this book? How is Jesus calling you to live differently as a result of this study?

  These questions are personal. Your answer should reflect on the main ideas expressed in this series and include a description of how your own understanding of Revelation has changed or deepened as a result of this teaching series.

REVIEW QUIZ

Lesson 24

1. **C.**
   In contrast to interpretive approaches that emphasize cutting and pasting verses from different books together or identifying each symbol with detailed specificity, Dr. Godfrey commended a literary approach that seeks to understand the overall flow of thought of each passage and to interpret details in light of that context.

2. **C.**
   Dr. Godfrey refers to 2 Peter 3:8 and Psalm 90:4 as two verses that use the imagery of one thousand years' being like a day to God in order to describe His relationship with time. Unlike human beings, God exists beyond time and is not bound to its limitations.

3. **A.**
   To refer to God as "eternal" is to say that He exists beyond time. This is an attribute of God that humans will never share. As part of our human existence in the new heaven and the new earth, we will continue to be bound by time—but by a time that will continue without end. Therefore, it is more accurate to describe this future state as everlasting life.

4. **B.**
   Orthodox Jews believe that the Messiah will establish the true state of Israel when he comes. Therefore, while Orthodox Jews celebrate the establishment of the current state of Israel in 1948 as a positive development, they do not ascribe any particular religious or prophetic significance to the state that currently exists.

5. **D.**
   Revelation presents battles, such as in Revelation 16:16, with tremendous brevity because its focus is not on the timing, tactics, or details of the battles but on the fact that God and His people are victorious.

6. **B.**
   Scripture provides few concrete details about the experiences of unbelievers between death and the final judgment, but Dr. Godfrey argued that the evidence we do have in Scripture strongly suggests that unbelievers experience a kind of provisional state of suffering that will be confirmed and intensified at the final judgment. This parallels believers' provisional state of rest and joy, which will also be confirmed and intensified at the final judgment.